marie claire

zesty

Thunder Bay Press
An imprint of the Advantage Publishers Group
5880 Oberlin Drive, San Diego, CA 92121-4794
www.thunderbaybooks.com

All notations of errors or omissions should be addressed to Thunder Bay Press, Editorial Department, at the above address. All other correspondence (author inquiries, permissions) concerning the content of this book should be addressed to Murdoch Books Pty Limited, Pier 8/9 23 Hickson Road, Millers Point NSW 2000 Australia.

Author and Stylist: Michele Cranston   Photographer: Petrina Tinslay
Design manager: Vivien Valk   Designer: Lauren Camilleri
Food preparation: Ross Dobson and Jo Glynn   Editor: Gordana Trifunovic
Production: Monika Paratore

ISBN-13: 978-1-59223-659-6
ISBN-10: 1-59223-659-6
Library of Congress Cataloging-in-Publication Data available upon request.

Printed by 1010 Printing. Printed in China.
1 2 3 4 5 10 09 08 07 06

IMPORTANT: Those who might be at risk from the effects of salmonella poisoning (the elderly, pregnant women, young children, and those suffering from immune deficiency diseases) should consult their doctor with any concerns about eating raw eggs.

CONVERSION GUIDE: You may find cooking times vary depending on the oven you are using. For convection ovens, as a general rule, set the oven temperature to 70°F lower than indicated in the recipe. We have used 4 teaspoon to 1 tablespoon measurements. If you are using a 3 teaspoon to 1 tablespoon measure, for most recipes the difference will not be noticeable. However, for recipes using baking powder, gelatin, baking soda, or small amounts of flour and cornstarch, add an extra teaspoon for each tablespoon specified.

marie claire

zesty

michele cranston
photography by petrina tinslay

THUNDER BAY
P · R · E · S · S
San Diego, California

contents

Welcome to *Marie Claire Zesty*, a selection of our favorite recipes that are warm and inviting, hot and spicy, rich and indulgent, or simply berry marvelous. We hope this thick and hearty book with lots of yummy ideas will inspire you with everything from simple tomato salads and chili salsas through warming stews and tempting chocolate cakes.

I've had a lot of fun revisiting old favorites, and I hope that you have as much fun cooking and eating from our selection.

michele cranston

ingredient note　　　　　# chilies

Hot and fiery, gently warming, or only for the brave, chilies come in a range of shapes, sizes, and colors, from the tiny bird's-eye chili to small and large bell shapes and on to the large Mexican-style chilies.

When using fresh chilies, choose those depending on your personal taste and heat tolerance. Remember that the smaller the chili, the hotter it is. If you don't like too much bite, then buy the large red chilies and always remove the seeds. However, it is always advisable to test a little of the chili because the heat factor will vary even within the larger chilies. If you like your food hot, then the small bird's-eye chilies are the ones for you. If you're feeling particularly brave, then leave the seeds intact. And remember that no matter how hot the chili, always wash your hands after preparing them, as a residue of the heat-inducing capsaicin will remain on your fingers long after you've finished slicing and chopping.

If you like hot and smoky flavors, then investigate some of the dried and canned Mexican chilies like the chipotle and ancho varieties.

tomatoes

There's nothing more disappointing than a cold and tasteless tomato. So remember these two basic rules: never store tomatoes in the refrigerator, and only use them when they are a rich, ruby red.

Nowadays, supermarkets and produce stands have an inspiring range available. If they are not perfectly red, allow them a couple of days on your kitchen counter before using. Think cherry tomatoes, multicolored pear tomatoes, baby and full-sized plum tomatoes, truss tomatoes, and vine-ripened tomatoes.

To enhance the flavor of fresh tomatoes, you can simply toss them with some sea salt, torn basil leaves, black olives, salted capers, anchovies, oregano, fresh baby mozzarella balls, or wild arugula leaves. Finish with a drizzle of extra-virgin olive oil and some balsamic vinegar and you'll have created the perfect side to a summery meal. Though superb in salads, don't forget they also make a great base for salsas, sauces, and casseroles.

ingredient note   # bell peppers

Bell peppers are one of those wonderfully useful vegetables
that can appear in a surprising range of meals. With their
full spectrum of colors—red, yellow, orange, and green—they
are the perfect vegetable when you want to add a dash of
color to a recipe. When finely cut into strips, they provide
the perfect crunch factor in salads or Asian stir-fries, and
when finely chopped, they bring a wonderful flavor to soups
and sauces.

Baked whole and filled with a richly flavored rice or meat
mixture, they're a satisfying mouthful of Mediterranean
comfort food. However, red bell peppers really come into
their own when roasted, broiled, or charbroiled on a barbecue.
Once roasted, the flesh becomes richly sweet. If chargrilled
the additional smokiness imparts a special background flavor
to many recipes. Roasted red bell peppers can be pureed into
a soup or dip, tossed with fresh herbs as a salsa, marinated
with fresh herbs and garlic as part of a salad or antipasto
plate, or added to the ingredients of a fritatta or pizza.

berries

Sweet strawberries, luscious raspberries, juicy mulberries, fat blueberries and tart red currants . . . who can say *no* to a bowl of such jeweled perfection? They can be served quite simply and still seem perfectly indulgent. Pile them into a bowl and sprinkle with a little sugar or dollop them with some rich cream—desserts don't come much easier.

Berries and cream are a combination made in heaven. Serve strawberries with whipped cream and crushed meringue, or mash the berries with a little sugar and liqueur and pour over vanilla ice cream. Cut strawberries into quarters and put in a bowl with a dash of balsamic vinegar. Gently fold the vinegar through the berries. Spoon the strawberries over a large dollop of mascarpone cheese and drizzle with a little honey.

Berries freeze well, so for a taste of summer in the cooler months, invest in some frozen berries. They'll make a great gelatin dessert, crumble, or sauce. They can also be folded through a basic cake mix for a rippled afternoon treat.

parmesan parchment bread chili hushpuppies oven-roasted tomatoes radishes with butter and wheat bread sautéed mushrooms seared beef and roasted tomato salsa crostini fresh mozzarella salad poached tomato with goat cheese chili cornbread fried haloumi pockets mini pies with white bean puree and cherry tomatoes octopus on toast marinated olives tomato and basil bruschetta olive

01 starters and sides

and pine nut crostini baguette with broiled goat cheese baby mozzarella and tomato in vine leaves greek salad cheese, chili, and olive quesadillas mango salsa with black beans tomato with chili and cilantro tomato relish goat cheese, prosciutto, and

parmesan parchment bread

makes 8

1¹/₂ tablespoons butter
1 cup finely chopped onion
1 teaspoon finely chopped rosemary
1 teaspoon salt
freshly ground black pepper, to season
¹/₂ cup all-purpose flour
2 tablespoons grated fresh Parmesan
　cheese
caponata, to serve (see basics)

Heat the butter in a small frying pan over medium heat. Add the onion and rosemary and cook, stirring, for 10 minutes or until the onion is slightly caramelized. Remove from the heat, season with salt and some freshly ground black pepper, and set aside to cool.

Preheat the oven to 300°F. In a food processor, pulse the flour and Parmesan until the mixture resembles bread crumbs. Gradually add the onion mixture and process until the dough just comes together.

Divide the dough into eighths and roll out each portion thinly between two sheets of floured parchment paper. Remove the top sheet from each and place the dough on cookie sheets. Bake in batches for 10 minutes or until golden brown, then turn over and bake for an additional 5 minutes or until crisp. Cool on a wire rack and break into pieces. Serve the parchment bread with caponata or a favorite dip.

marinated olives

makes 2³/₄ cups

2³/₄ cups mixed olives
4 long strips orange zest
2 garlic cloves, crushed
1 red chili, seeded
a few thyme sprigs
3 tablespoons extra-virgin olive oil

Put the olives in a bowl. Add the orange zest, garlic, chili, and thyme. Pour over the oil and toss to combine. Cover the olives and allow to marinate in the refrigerator overnight.

radishes with butter and wheat bread

serves 6

1 ripe tomato
1/2 cup butter, softened
1 teaspoon sea salt
2 bunches small radishes
6 slices wheat bread, to serve

Remove the seeds from the tomato and finely dice the flesh. Place in a bowl along with the softened butter and sea salt. Stir to combine and place into a small dish. Serve alongside the radishes with some thinly sliced wheat bread.

fresh mozzarella salad

serves 4

four 4¹/₂-ounce balls fresh mozzarella
  cheese
4 tablespoons extra-virgin olive oil
1 large handful sage leaves
20 large black olives, pitted
  and quartered
1 orange, zested and juiced

Cut the mozzarella into thick slices and arrange them on four plates. Put the oil in a frying pan over high heat and add the sage leaves. As they begin to sizzle and darken, remove them from the oil and scatter them over the cheese. Gently pour a little of the oil over the mozzarella, then top with the olive quarters, orange zest, and orange juice. Serve with toasted focaccia or ciabatta.

tomato and basil bruschetta

makes 8 pieces

8 ripe tomatoes
sea salt and frshly ground black
  pepper, to season
8 thick slices country-style bread
1 garlic clove, lightly crushed
a few basil leaves, torn
olive oil, to drizzle

Cut the tomatoes in half and scoop out most of the seeds. Discard the seeds and finely dice the flesh. Put the tomato into a bowl and season liberally with sea salt and freshly ground black pepper.

Broil or toast the bread on both sides. Rub the top of each toasted slice with the garlic. Put the diced tomato onto the toast and top with torn basil leaves. Drizzle with olive oil and serve.

olive and pine nut crostini

makes 12 pieces

3 tablespoons red wine vinegar
6 anchovies
2 garlic cloves
3/4 cup pine nuts, toasted
2 teaspoons salted capers, rinsed
   and drained
4 hard-boiled egg yolks
12 large green olives, pitted
1 small handful Italian parsley,
   finely chopped
1 baguette, cut into 12 thin slices
olive oil
1/4 cup crumbled goat cheese or
   shaved Parmesan cheese
freshly ground black pepper, to season

Preheat the oven to 300°F. Put the vinegar, anchovy fillets, garlic, pine nuts, capers, egg yolks, and olives into a food processor. Process to a smooth paste and spoon into a bowl. Add the parsley to the bowl and stir in. Brush one side of each baguette slice with olive oil. Put the slices on a baking sheet and bake until golden brown, turning once. Spoon the topping onto the crostini slices and top with some crumbled goat cheese or shaved Parmesan cheese. Season with freshly ground black pepper.

seared beef and roasted tomato salsa crostini

makes about 30 pieces

4 plum tomatoes, quartered
1 teaspoon sugar
1 teaspoon salt
10 basil leaves, shredded
10 mint leaves, shredded
1 teaspoon balsamic vinegar
10$\frac{1}{2}$-ounce piece tenderloin steak,
   about 1$\frac{1}{2}$ inches in diameter
freshly ground black pepper, to season
1 tablespoon vegetable oil
sea salt, to season
1 baguette, thinly sliced, to serve

Preheat the oven to 315°F. Place the tomato quarters in a roasting pan and sprinkle evenly with the sugar and salt. Bake for about 40 minutes or until the tomatoes begin to blacken on the edges and dry out. Remove from the heat and allow to cool. Slice the roasted tomatoes thinly and place in a bowl with the shredded basil and mint leaves. Add the balsamic vinegar and mix well to combine.

Season the beef tenderloin steak with freshly ground black pepper. Heat the oil in a frying pan over high heat and sear the steak for 2 minutes on all sides. Remove from the heat and sprinkle with a little sea salt. Set aside to cool, then slice into 1/2-inch thick widths. Place on the baguette slices and top with the tomato salsa.

chili corn bread

makes approximately 24 pieces

1 cup cornmeal
1 cup all-purpose flour
1 tablespoon baking powder
1 tablespoon sugar
3 eggs, lightly beaten
3/4 cup milk
2 tablespoons plain yogurt
3 tablespoons olive oil
3/4 cup corn kernels
1/2 red bell pepper, diced
1 small red chili, seeded and chopped
3 teaspoons finely chopped marjoram
5 scallions, thinly sliced
salt and freshly ground black pepper,
   to season
1/2 cup grated mozzarella cheese

Place the cornmeal, flour, baking powder, and sugar in a bowl. Make a well in the center and add the eggs, milk, yogurt, and oil. Mix well. Add the corn, bell pepper, chili, marjoram, and scallions. Mix well. Season with salt and freshly ground black pepper.

Preheat the oven to 350°F. Pour the batter into a greased 12 x 8-inch shallow baking pan and top with the mozzarella. Bake for 35 minutes or until a skewer comes out clean when inserted into the center. Cool slightly in the pan, then turn out onto a clean work surface. Trim the sides and cut into 1 1/2-inch squares.

tartlets with white bean puree and cherry tomatoes

makes 30

1/2 cup dried white beans, soaked
  overnight
2 garlic cloves
30 cherry tomatoes
1 1/2 tablespoons lemon thyme sprigs
1/2 cup olive oil
2 1/2 teaspoons salt
salt and freshly ground black pepper,
  to season
30 prebaked short-crust tartlet
  shells (see basics)

Drain the beans and place them with the garlic cloves in a saucepan filled with water. Bring to a boil and simmer for 30 minutes.

Meanwhile, preheat the oven to 350°F. Place the cherry tomatoes in a baking pan with 2 teaspoons of the lemon thyme, 1/4 cup of the olive oil, and about 1/2 teaspoon of salt. Bake for 30 minutes.

Add 2 teaspoons of salt to the white beans in the last 5 minutes of their cooking time. Check that the beans are soft, then drain. Mash by hand or in a food processor with the remaining thyme and olive oil. Season to taste with salt and freshly ground black pepper.

Fill each of the tartlet shells with a teaspoon of the white beans and top with one of the roasted cherry tomatoes. Serve immediately.

octopus on toast makes 32 pieces

8 small octopus, cleaned
2 tablespoons red wine vinegar
1 teaspoon dried oregano
1 cup olive oil
8 thick slices white bread, crusts
  removed
4 garlic cloves
1 teaspoon salt
3 potatoes, boiled and mashed
1 tablespoon lemon juice
2 tablespoons finely chopped Italian
  parsley
1 tablespoon pitted and finely
  chopped black olives
2 teaspoons seeded and finely
  chopped red chili
1 teaspoon finely chopped lemon zest

Place the octopus in a ceramic or glass bowl. Combine the vinegar, oregano, and 1/4 cup of the oil. Pour over the octopus. Cover and leave to marinate for 30 minutes.

Preheat the oven to 350°F. Cut each slice of bread into quarters. Place on a baking sheet and toast in the oven until golden. Remove and allow to cool on a wire rack.

To make the sauce, place the garlic and salt in a mortar and pestle and grind until soft and creamy. Place in a bowl and add the mashed potatoes and lemon juice. Whisk the mixture continuously while slowly adding the remaining olive oil. When the sauce is light and fluffy, fold in the parsley, olives, chili, and lemon zest.

Heat a heavy-based frying pan over high heat and sear the octopus for 2–3 minutes on both sides until colored. Remove and cut into quarters. Place a heaping tablespoon of the sauce on each of the bread squares and top with the octopus.

fried haloumi pockets

5 sheets phyllo pastry, cut in half to
   form squares
2 ripe tomatoes
1/3 cup butter, melted
10 slices haloumi cheese or other
   semihard, salty sheep cheese
20 Italian parsley leaves
10 large mint leaves
freshly ground black pepper, to season

Cover the pastry sheets with a damp cloth. Cut the tomatoes in half, then slice to form thin wedges. Lightly brush one of the sheets of phyllo with butter and fold in half to form a rectangle. Lightly butter the top, then place a slice of haloumi in the center. Top with three wedges of tomato, two parsley leaves, a mint leaf, and a sprinkle of freshly ground black pepper. Fold the sides in on the haloumi and then roll up. Repeat the process with the remaining ingredients. Grease a large frying pan and cook the pockkets over medium heat until the undersides are golden brown, then flip over to cook the other side. Serve warm, either whole or cut in half.

baguette with broiled goat cheese
serves 4

1 baguette
4 slices goat cheese
dressed salad of baby leaves
1 handful olives
1 handful pomegranate seeds
4 marinated artichoke hearts, chopped
freshly ground black pepper, to season

Slice the baguette diagonally into four long thin slices. Lightly toast the slices, then top with the goat cheese. Broil until the cheese is golden brown. Serve on a dressed salad of baby leaves. Add the olives, pomegranate seeds, and artichoke hearts. Season with freshly ground black pepper.

goat cheese, prosciutto, and sour cherries on rye

makes 15 pieces

5 slices rye bread, crusts removed
1/2 cup fresh goat cheese
5 slices prosciutto, each slice cut
   into three pieces
1/4 cup finely chopped bottled
   sour cherries
freshly ground black pepper, to season

Cut each slice of bread into three fingers. Spread a little of the goat cheese onto each piece of bread and top with a piece of prosciutto and a teaspoon of chopped sour cherries. Serve immediately with a sprinkle of freshly ground black pepper.

broiled oysters
makes 24

1¹/2 ounces pancetta, finely diced
¹/2 cup fresh bread crumbs
2 tablespoons finely chopped
   Italian parsley
1¹/2 tablespoons unsalted butter,
   melted
¹/2 teaspoon Tabasco sauce
1 tablespoon Worcestershire sauce
24 oysters
lemon wedges, to serve

Place the pancetta, bread crumbs, and parsley in a small bowl and mix well. Add the melted butter, Tabasco sauce, and Worcestershire sauce and fold through. Spread a teaspoon of the mixture over each oyster and place under a hot broiler for 2 minutes or until the topping is golden brown. Remove from the heat and serve with wedges of lemon.

tomato salsa

4 plum tomatoes, thinly diced
10 basil leaves, thinly sliced
2 tablespoons finely diced red onion
1/2 teaspoon very finely chopped garlic
3 tablespoons extra-virgin olive oil
1 tablespoon balsamic vinegar
1/2 teaspoon sea salt

Put the tomatoes into a bowl. Add the basil, onion, garlic, oil, balsamic vinegar, and sea salt. Stir to combine. Check the seasoning; you may wish to add a little more salt to taste.

Serve with broiled tuna, swordfish, or cod. It can also be served with spicy marinated chicken or seared lamb.

mushroom and pancetta bruschetta

makes 8 pieces

2 tablespoons butter
6 pieces pancetta, thinly sliced
2¹/4 cups thinly sliced button
  mushrooms
2¹/4 cups oyster mushrooms,
  thinly sliced
sea salt freshly ground black pepper,
  to season
8 thick slices country-style bread
1 garlic clove, lightly crushed
shaved Parmesan cheese, to serve

Heat the butter in a frying pan over medium heat. As the butter melts, add the pancetta. Cook for 1 minute, then stir in the mushrooms. Cover the pan and reduce the heat to low. Cook the mushrooms for 5 minutes, then remove from the heat. Season to taste with a little sea salt and freshly ground black pepper.

Broil or toast the bread on both sides. Rub the top of each toasted slice with the garlic clove. Spoon the cooked mushrooms onto the bread slices. Top with the Parmesan cheese.

cheese, chili, and olive
quesadillas   makes 24 or 48 pieces

1/4 cup pitted black olives, chopped
1 large red chili, seeded and chopped
1/2 cup olive oil
21/4 cups grated mozzarella cheese
1 cup grated feta cheese
twelve 8-inch tortillas
21/2 cups cilantro leaves

Preheat the oven to 350°F. Place the olives, chili, and oil in a blender and blend to form a flavored oil. Set aside. Place the grated mozzarella and feta in a bowl and toss to combine.

Place one of the tortillas on a baking sheet. Sprinkle with a coating of the mixed cheeses and some cilantro leaves. Cover with a second tortilla and brush well with the oil mixture. Continue making quesadillas with the remaining ingredients. Bake for about 7 minutes. Turn the quesadillas over and cook for an additional 8 minutes. Remove the quesadillas from the oven and slice into quarters or eighths. Serve immediately.

avocado with chili salsa

serves 4

2 avocados
2 limes
sea salt and freshly ground black
  pepper, to season
1 tablespoon finely chopped red onion
8 cherry tomatoes, finely chopped
1 red chili, seeded and finely chopped
1 tablespoon finely chopped cilantro
  leaves
2 tablespoons extra-virgin olive oil
1 teaspoon smoked paprika
1 handful cilantro leaves
4 small white corn tortillas, toasted

Slice the avocados in half lengthwise. Remove the seeds and scoop out the whole flesh with a large spoon. Put the avocado halves onto a plate and finely slice to form a fan. Squeeze half a lime over each avocado half and season with sea salt and freshly ground black pepper. Combine the onion, tomatoes, chili, and chopped cilantro in a bowl, then sprinkle over the avocado. Finish off with a drizzle of olive oil and a sprinkle of paprika. Garnish with the cilantro leaves and serve with the toasted tortillas.

greek salad

4 ripe tomatoes, cut into chunks
2 short cucumbers, thickly cut
1/2 red onion, sliced into paper-thin
   half rings
1 cup kalamata olives
1/4 teaspoon dried oregano
7 ounces creamy feta cheese,
   thickly sliced

dressing
1 teaspoon red wine vinegar
2–3 tablespoons extra-virgin olive oil

Arrange the tomatoes on a serving platter. Add the cucumbers and onion. Sprinkle with the olives and oregano. Put the feta slices on top of the salad. Combine the dressing ingredients and drizzle over the salad.

baby mozzarella and tomato in vine leaves makes 24 wraps

24 packaged vine leaves
2 plum tomatoes, finely diced
7 ounces fresh baby mozzarella
   cheese, diced (about 17 balls)
24 large mint leaves
freshly ground black pepper, to season
olive oil, for frying
lemon wedges, to serve

Unwrap the vine leaves and soak them for 1 hour in a large bowl filled with boiling water. Remove and gently pat dry. Place a row of diced tomato at one end of each vine leaf. Top with some of the diced baby mozzarella, a mint leaf, and some freshly ground black pepper. Roll up firmly, folding the edges in as you go. Heat a large frying pan with a little oil and fry each of the wraps for 1 minute on each side. Serve warm with a squeeze of lemon.

tomato and cheese tarts

makes 6

8 plum tomatoes, cut into
  eight wedges
salt and freshly ground black pepper,
  to season
1 cup heavy cream
3 eggs
1 cup grated Gruyère cheese
1¹/₂ cups grated Parmesan cheese
6 prebaked 3¹/₄-inch short-crust
  tartlet shells (see basics)
2 tablespoons oregano
18 basil leaves, roughly torn
1 tablespoon extra-virgin olive oil

Preheat the oven to 350°F. Put the tomatoes on a baking sheet, sprinkle with salt and freshly ground black pepper, and bake for 30 minutes.

Whisk together the cream, eggs, Gruyère, and Parmesan cheese. Pour the mixture into the tartlet shells. Bake for 20 minutes or until the eggs are set and the filling is golden brown.

Put the tomatoes in a small bowl with the oregano, basil, and olive oil. Toss together. Pile the tomato mixture on top of each tartlet. Serve as is or on a bed of leafy greens.

prosciutto, mozzarella, and tomato wraps

makes 20

2 plum tomatoes
20 thin slices prosciutto
20 slices mozzarella cheese
freshly ground black pepper, to season

Slice each tomato into ten vertical slices and then cut the slices in half horizontally. Lay a slice of prosciutto on the work surface. Place one halved slice of tomato on it, followed by a slice of mozzarella and then another slice of tomato. Season with freshly ground black pepper and roll up firmly to make a little wrap. Repeat with the remaining ingredients. Heat a lightly greased frying pan over medium heat and cook the prosciutto wraps for 2–3 minutes or until golden brown.

broiled mushrooms

8 field mushrooms
3 garlic cloves, finely chopped
1 teaspoon red chili flakes
1/2 cup extra-virgin olive oil
sea salt, to season
8 slices ciabatta bread, toasted
1 handful arugula
1 handful Italian parsley

Put the mushrooms, stalk side up, on a baking sheet. Combine the garlic, chili flakes, and extra-virgin olive oil in a small bowl. Spoon the flavored oil over the mushrooms and season with a little sea salt.

Place the mushrooms under a hot broiler and cook for 10 minutes, then remove from the heat. Put the toasted ciabatta onto four plates. Add some arugula, top with the mushrooms, sprinkle with the parsley, and drizzle with the cooking liquid.

red and green sauce

makes 1 cup

red sauce

4 plum tomatoes, quartered
1 teaspoon sugar
1 teaspoon sea salt
1 tablespoon pomegranate molasses
10 basil leaves
1 garlic clove
1 teaspoon ground cumin
salt and freshly ground black pepper,
  to season

Preheat the oven to 350°F. Place the tomato pieces on a baking sheet and sprinkle evenly with the sugar and sea salt. Roast for 40 minutes or until the tomatoes begin to blacken at the edges and dry out. Place the tomatoes in a food processor or blender with the remaining ingredients and blend to form a smooth sauce. Season with salt and freshly ground black pepper.

green sauce

3 handfuls Italian parsley
30 mint leaves
5 anchovies
1 tablespoon Indian lime pickle
3 teaspoons lemon juice
1/2 cup olive oil

Place all the ingredients in a blender or food processor. Blend until smooth.

Note—These sauces can be used to accompany broiled lamb chops, and each is sufficient to serve with 10–12 chops. Serve both sauces at room temperature.

poached tomatoes with goat cheese

serves 4

4 large vine-ripened tomatoes
8 peppercorns
1 1/2 teaspoons sea salt
1 tablespoon balsamic vinegar
1/2 red onion, thinly sliced
6 sprigs parsley
2 1/4 cups arugula
1/3 cup pesto (see basics)
3/4 cup crumbled goat cheese

Preheat the oven to 350°F. Put the tomatoes in a small, deep baking dish, then fill the dish with enough water to come halfway up the side of the tomatoes. Add the peppercorns, sea salt, vinegar, onion, and parsley sprigs. Bake for 40 minutes.

Divide the arugula among four plates. Lift the tomatoes out of the dish, arrange on top of the arugula, and drizzle each with some of the cooking liquid. Add some pesto and crumbled goat cheese and serve.

tomatoes with chili and cilantro

serves 4

2²/₃ cups cilantro leaves,
  roughly chopped
1 red onion, finely diced
2 large red chilies, seeded and
  finely chopped
1 teaspoon sea salt
3 tablespoons olive oil
1 tablespoon balsamic vinegar
4 large ripe tomatoes

Put the cilantro, onion, chilies, sea salt, olive oil, and balsamic vinegar in a bowl and toss together.

Slice the tomatoes and arrange them on a plate. Scatter the cilantro salsa on top, season, and serve as a side dish or as a salad with a little seared tuna or fresh ricotta.

chili hush puppies   makes 20

3/4 cup all-purpose flour
1 teaspoon baking powder
1 egg
11/2 tablespoons butter, melted
1/2 teaspoon salt
3 tablespoons milk
1 teaspoon Tabasco sauce
2 corncobs, kernels removed
   (approximately 2 cups)
1/3 cup vegetable oil

Place the flour, baking powder, egg, melted butter, and salt in a mixing bowl and stir together. Add the milk and Tabasco sauce to form a thick batter, then add the fresh corn. Heat the oil in a frying pan over medium heat. Drop small spoonfuls of the batter into the oil in batches and fry each side until golden brown. Remove and drain on paper towels. Serve warm with a sweet chili sauce.

chili butternut
quesadillas

1/3 cup pitted and chopped
  black olives
1 large red chili, seeded and chopped
1/2 cup olive oil
1/2 small butternut squash
1 teaspoon smoked paprika
2 cups grated mozzarella cheese
1 cup crumbled feta cheese
ten 61/4-inch white corn tortillas
3 cups cilantro leaves

Preheat the oven to 350°F. Put the olives, chili, and oil into a blender and blend to form a flavored oil. Dice the squash into small pieces and put onto a baking sheet. Brush with a little of the chili oil. Sprinkle with the paprika. Bake for 30 minutes or until golden brown and soft. Put the cheeses into a small bowl and toss to combine.

Place one tortilla on a clean work surface. Sprinkle with a liberal coating of the mixed cheeses, some of the roasted squash, and a scattering of cilantro leaves. Cover with a second tortilla, brush well with the flavored oil, and set aside. Repeat the process with the remaining ingredients. Put the quesadillas onto an oiled baking sheet and bake for 7 minutes. Turn the quesadillas over and cook for an additional 7–8 minutes. Remove from the oven and slice into quarters.

tuna and red bell pepper skewers
makes 20

18-ounce tuna fillet
1 tablespoon olive oil
1 teaspoon ground coriander
2 teaspoons ground cumin
1 red bell pepper
20 small skewers, soaked in hot water
    for 20 minutes
salt and freshly ground black pepper,
    to season

lemon mayonnaise
2 egg yolks
1 lemon, zest grated, juiced
1 cup vegetable oil
salt and white pepper, to season
1 tablespoon finely chopped preserved
    lemon
1 tablespoon finely chopped cilantro
    leaves
2 tablespoons lime juice

Cut the tuna into 3/4-inch cubes and place in a bowl. Add the oil, ground coriander, and ground cumin. Mix together. Set aside and allow to marinate for 1 hour. Preheat the oven to 350°F.

To make the lemon mayonnaise, whisk the egg yolks, grated zest, and lemon juice together in a bowl. Slowly drizzle in the oil, whisking the mixture until it becomes thick and creamy. Season with salt and white pepper. Place the mayonnaise in a small bowl and stir in the preserved lemon, cilantro leaves, and lime juice.

Slice the bell pepper into 3/4-inch squares. Ease on two alternate pieces of tuna and bell pepper per skewer. Place on a baking sheet and bake for 5–7 minutes. Season with salt and freshly ground black pepper. Serve with the lemon mayonnaise.

mango salsa with black beans

serves 4

1¹/₄ cups canned Chinese black beans
1 mango, diced
1 teaspoon ground cumin
1 large red chili, seeded and
   finely chopped
3 tablespoons lime juice
1 teaspoon sesame oil
2 scallions, thinly sliced
1 large handful cilantro leaves
salt and pepper, to season

Rinse the black beans, drain them, and put them in a large bowl. Add the remaining ingredients, stir to combine, and season to taste. Serve as a side salad or with barbecued chicken.

tomato relish

makes 3 cups

12 tomatoes, coarsely chopped
1 red onion, thinly sliced
3 garlic cloves, finely chopped
1 tablespoon finely grated fresh ginger
1/2 teaspoon ground allspice
2 teaspoons yellow mustard seeds
1/4 teaspoon red chili powder
2 teaspoons sea salt
2/3 cup white wine vinegar
11/4 cups sugar

Put the tomatoes, onion, garlic, ginger, allspice, mustard seeds, chili powder, sea salt, and white wine vinegar into a large saucepan. Bring to a boil. Simmer covered for 1 hour before adding the sugar. Remove the cover and simmer for 40 minutes, stirring occasionally. Carefully pour into sterilized jars and allow to cool before storing. Serve as a condiment on ham or cheddar sandwiches or spooned over broiled lamb.

roasted red bell peppers

serves 2

4 red bell peppers
2 tablespoons olive oil
salt and pepper, to season

Preheat the oven to 400°F. Place a small rack on or over a baking sheet or roasting pan. Lightly rub the bell peppers with olive oil and place on the rack. Bake until the skin begins to blister and blacken. Turn the bell peppers several times during baking so that the skin blisters all over.

Remove the bell peppers from the oven and put in a container. Cover with plastic wrap and allow to cool.

Remove the blackened skin from the bell peppers by gently rubbing it away with your fingers. The skin should come away easily. Remove the stems and the seeds from inside the bell peppers. Lay the cleaned flesh on a board and finely slice or chop it.

Season and toss with a little olive oil before serving with barbecued tuna or swordfish, or spiced chicken. Mix with some pitted olives and serve with roast beef or broiled lamb. If not using right away, you can marinate the bell peppers in olive oil with garlic and basil leaves.

sautéed mushrooms

serves 4

6 cups cremini mushrooms
3 tablespoons butter
1 garlic clove, finely chopped
sea salt and freshly ground black
    pepper, to season

Put the mushrooms in a pan with the butter, garlic, and a little sea salt. Heat over medium heat. When the butter begins to sizzle, cover with a lid and reduce the heat to low. Cook for 10 minutes, then remove from the heat. Season with freshly ground black pepper before serving.

Serve with scrambled eggs and crispy bacon or as a side for broiled steak.

tapenade

makes 1 cup

1/2 cup pitted kalamata olives
1 garlic clove
1 handful roughly chopped
   Italian parsley
10 basil leaves
2 anchovy fillets
1 teaspoon capers, rinsed and drained
3 tablespoons olive oil
freshly ground black pepper, to season

Put the olives, garlic, parsley, basil, anchovies, and capers into a blender or food processor and blend to a rough paste. Add the olive oil in a stream until you reach the desired consistency. Season with freshly ground black pepper to taste.

Serve as a dollop on barbecued tuna or lamb fillets or spread on crusty white bread and serve with sliced tomatoes and salami.

oven-roasted tomatoes

serves 2

2 plum tomatoes
a few thyme sprigs
**sea salt and freshly ground black
  pepper, to season**
extra-virgin olive oil, to drizzle

Preheat the oven to 350°F. Slice the tomatoes in half lengthwise and put in a roasting pan lined with parchment paper. Scatter with the thyme sprigs and season liberally with sea salt and freshly ground black pepper. Drizzle with a little extra-virgin olive oil and bake for 40 minutes.

Serve with creamy scrambled eggs, broiled sausages, or barbecued tuna.

artichoke, oregano, and prosciutto pizza red bell pepper salad red onion tart warm salad of fennel and salami cumin tortillas with roasted bell pepper romano pizza warm leek salad fresh tomato and oregano salad pan bagna matsutake mushroom salad white bean salad roasted bell pepper and green olive salad chili corn cakes pissaladière sardines on toast summer salad with spiced goat cheese

02 light meals

black bean salsa with tortillas broiled polenta with mushrooms jeweled gazpacho prosciutto and snap pea salad niçoise salad roasted squash salad margherita pizza marinated seared shrimp with bruschetta mushrooms baked in vine leaves three bean salad with

artichoke, oregano, and prosciutto pizza

makes 4

2 vine-ripened tomatoes
sea salt, to season
4 tablespoons olive oil
1 quantity pizza dough (see basics)
8 slices prosciutto, cut in half
3/4 cup marinated artichoke hearts,
   drained and sliced
3/4 cup crumbled goat cheese
a few oregano leaves, to garnish

Preheat the oven to 400°F. Cut the tomatoes into eighths and put them onto a baking sheet. Season with sea salt and drizzle with 2 tablespoons of the olive oil. Roast the tomatoes for 15 minutes. Remove from the oven.

Roll out four small rounds of the pizza dough, each one about 41/2 inches in diameter. Put onto a baking sheet and top with the prosciutto, roasted tomatoes, artichoke hearts, and goat cheese. Drizzle with a little olive oil and season with sea salt. Bake for 15 minutes, then garnish with a few oregano leaves.

red bell pepper salad

serves 4

2 red bell peppers
2 garlic cloves, thinly sliced
4 anchovies, finely chopped
4 small ripe plum tomatoes, halved
4 tablespoons olive oil
sea salt and freshly ground black
  pepper, to season
1 handful Italian parsley
2 heads Belgian endive, washed and
  thinly sliced
2 hard-boiled eggs, finely chopped
1 tablespoon salted capers, rinsed
  and drained

Preheat the oven to 400°F. Cut the bell peppers in half and remove any seeds. Put the bell pepper halves, open side up, on a baking sheet. Scatter with the garlic and anchovies. Place a tomato half inside each bell pepper half. Drizzle with the olive oil and season with sea salt and freshly ground black pepper. Bake for 1 hour.

Divide the parsley and Belgian endive among four plates. Put a bell pepper half on each plate. Sprinkle with the chopped egg and capers. Drizzle with the pan juices and serve immediately.

red onion tart

serves 8

1¹/₂ sheets butter puff pastry
2 tablespoons butter
1 large pinch saffron threads
6 red onions, thinly sliced
¹/₂ cup white wine
1 heaping teaspoon sea salt
1 teaspoon cracked black pepper
4 egg yolks
1 cup heavy cream
¹/₂ cup grated Parmesan cheese

Preheat the oven to 350°F. Line a 10-inch flan pan with the pastry and chill until needed.

Heat the butter and saffron in a large frying pan over medium heat. Add the onions and cook, stirring often, until they are soft and transparent. Pour in the white wine, cover the pan, and simmer on low heat for an additional 40 minutes or until the onions are buttery soft and slightly caramelized.

Prick the pastry base with a fork and add baking weights or uncooked rice. Bake blind for 15 minutes. Remove the baking weights or rice and bake for an additional 5–10 minutes or until the pastry is golden.

When the onions are cooked, add the salt and pepper and tip the mixture into the tart shell. Whisk the yolks and cream together and pour over the onions. Sprinkle with the Parmesan cheese and bake for 30 minutes or until the filling has set and is golden brown. Serve with a salad of bitter leaves.

warm salad of fennel and salami

serves 4

2 small fennel bulbs
10 thyme sprigs
4 tablespoons extra-virgin olive oil
salt and pepper, to season
2 tablespoons balsamic vinegar
16 slices spicy salami
2³/4 cups arugula
1 cup crumbled creamy feta cheese

Preheat the oven to 350°F. Slice the fennel bulbs lengthwise into quarters or eighths, depending on how big they are and put them on a baking sheet. Add the thyme and olive oil. Toss everything together, season well, and then cover with foil and bake for 30 minutes.

When the fennel has cooked through, drizzle it with the balsamic vinegar. Lay the salami slices on a cookie sheet and put them under the broiler for 2–3 minutes or until slightly crisp. Arrange the arugula on four plates and top with the fennel, salami, and crumbled feta.

cumin tortillas with roasted bell pepper

makes 12

tortillas

2 1/2 cups all-purpose flour
1/2 teaspoon baking powder
2 teaspoons ground cumin
1/3 cup canola oil
1 tablespoon lime juice
2/3 cup plain yogurt
1/2 teaspoon salt

roasted bell pepper filling

2 roasted red bell peppers,
  skinned and seeds removed, sliced
  into thin strips
10 basil leaves, torn
1 tablespoon balsamic vinegar
1 teaspoon salt
12-ounce tuna fillet, sliced lengthwise
  into three pieces

Sift the flour, baking powder, and cumin into a large bowl. Add the oil and mix well to form a dough. In a bowl, combine the lime juice, yogurt, and salt. Drizzle over the flour and slowly combine until the dough begins to soften. Gather into a ball and lightly knead until smooth. Divide into 12 portions. Taking one portion at a time, roll out on a floured surface to form a very thin 7-inch circle. Set aside and repeat with the remaining portions, placing plastic wrap or parchment paper between each tortilla.

Heat a large frying pan over medium heat. Cook the tortillas, turning once, so that each side is golden brown. Remove and keep warm by covering with a dishtowel.

Toss the roasted bell pepper with the basil, vinegar, and salt. Quickly sear the tuna fillet on all sides, then thinly slice. Place some of the roasted bell pepper filling on the tortillas, top with the tuna, roll up, and serve.

romano pizza

serves 4

18 ounces fresh baby mozzarella
  cheese (about 42 balls)
2 medium pizza bases (see basics)
6 anchovies, roughly chopped
extra-virgin olive oil, to drizzle
sea salt, to season
basil leaves, to serve

Preheat the oven to 400°F. Spread half of the cheese over the two pizza bases. Scatter half of the anchovies over the bases. Bake for 15 minutes. Remove from the oven and top with the remaining cheese and anchovies. Drizzle with the extra-virgin olive oil, season with a little sea salt, and return to the oven. Bake until the cheese has just melted. Sprinkle with the basil leaves before serving.

warm leek salad   serves 4

1 generous pinch saffron
1/4 cup butter
1/2 cup white wine
24 baby leeks
4 slices prosciutto
1 tablespoon olive oil
12 sage leaves
16 niçoise olives
1/2 cup creamy blue cheese
1 tablespoon small capers, rinsed
   and drained

Preheat the oven to 350°F. Place a deep roasting pan over high heat and sprinkle in the saffron, letting it heat through before adding the butter. As the butter sizzles, add the wine and leeks. Remove the pan from the heat, cover with foil, and bake for 40 minutes.

Meanwhile, heat a frying pan and cook the prosciutto until it is crisp and golden. Drain on paper towels. Add the olive oil to the pan and fry the sage leaves. When they begin to turn crisp, remove and drain on paper towels. Toss the olives in the hot oil and then remove the pan from the heat, leaving the olives in the pan.

When the leeks are cooked, arrange on four warmed plates. Top with the prosciutto, cheese, capers, sage, and olives. Pour over some of the juices from the frying pan and the roasting pan and serve.

fresh tomato and oregano salad

serves 4

1 small onion, halved and thinly sliced
2 teaspoons white sugar
1 tablespoon white wine vinegar
2 vine-ripened tomatoes
sea salt and freshly ground black
  pepper, to season
1 large handful oregano
extra-virgin olive oil, to drizzle

Toss the onion and sugar together and allow to stand for 30 minutes before adding the vinegar. Cut the tomatoes into eighths and sprinkle them with sea salt and freshly ground black pepper.

Just before serving the salad, toss the tomatoes, onion, and oregano leaves together and add a drizzle of extra-virgin olive oil.

pan bagna

1 thin baguette

1 tablespoon virgin olive oil

1 garlic clove, peeled and sliced in half

2 red bell peppers, roasted, skin and
   seeds removed

1 tablespoon salted capers, rinsed
   and drained

3/4 cup canned tuna, drained

15 black olives, pitted

1/2 small red onion, thinly sliced

15 basil leaves

1 large handful Italian parsley,
   roughly chopped

10 anchovies

1/2 cup marinated artichoke hearts,
   drained and sliced

salt and freshly ground black pepper,
   to season

With a sharp bread knife, slice the baguette in half down its length and remove the bread filling from both the top and bottom portions. Brush the interior of the loaf with olive oil and rub with garlic.

Cut the roasted bell pepper into thin strips and combine with the remaining ingredients in a bowl. Season with salt and freshly ground black pepper. Spoon inside the bottom half of the loaf, heaping it up. Reassemble the loaf, making sure that the sides meet neatly. Wrap in plastic wrap, put a weight on top (a breadboard or heavy saucepan is suitable) and put in the refrigerator overnight. Slice into 3/4-inch widths and serve.

salad of sweet onions and prosciutto

serves 4

2 tablespoons olive oil
8 slices prosciutto, halved
12 scallions, trimmed and halved
3 tablespoons thyme
1 tablespoon light brown sugar
2 tablespoons balsamic vinegar
1/2 cup red wine
2 ripe tomatoes, finely diced
sea salt and freshly ground black
    pepper, to season
1 head radicchio, trimmed, leaves
    washed
4 slices rye bread, toasted
2 tablespoons extra-virgin olive oil

Heat the olive oil in a large frying pan over medium heat and fry the prosciutto until lightly crisp. Drain on paper towels.

Add the scallions and thyme sprigs to the pan. Reduce the heat to low, sprinkle with the sugar, then add the vinegar and wine. Cover and cook slowly for 10 minutes.

Put the tomatoes in a bowl. Season with sea salt and freshly ground black pepper. Put the radicchio over the scallions for a few minutes or until it begins to wilt, then remove. Toss the scallions and tomatoes together.

To assemble, put the rye toast on four plates. Top with the radicchio, spoon over the tomato and scallions, then top with the prosciutto. Drizzle with the extra-virgin olive oil and serve immediately.

margherita pizza   serves 4

1³/4 cups canned plum tomatoes
2 tablespoons extra-virgin olive oil,
   plus extra for drizzling
2 medium pizza bases (see basics)
sea salt, to season
9 ounces fresh baby mozzarella
   cheese, sliced (about 20 balls)
2 tablespoons grated Parmesan
   cheese
oregano leaves, to serve

Preheat the oven to 400°F. Drain and finely chop the tomatoes. Put the tomatoes in a saucepan with the 2 tablespoons of oil and simmer over medium heat for 5 minutes or until the tomatoes are no longer watery. Allow to cool. Spread the tomato evenly over the pizza bases. Season with a little sea salt, drizzle with a little of the oil, and bake for 15 minutes. Remove from the oven and top with the baby mozzarella and Parmesan cheese. Return to the oven for a few minutes or until the cheese has melted. Top with the oregano leaves.

matsutake mushroom salad

2 garlic bulbs
3 tablespoons extra-virgin olive oil
1 tablespoon balsamic vinegar
salt and white pepper, to season
a pinch sugar
4 large matsutake mushrooms
2 tablespoons light olive oil
1/4 cup pine nuts, toasted
2 large handfuls Italian parsley,
   roughly chopped
1/3 cup shaved Parmesan cheese
1 sourdough baguette

Preheat the oven to 400°F. Wrap the garlic bulbs in foil and bake them in the oven for 30 minutes or until the cloves are soft and a little mushy. Slice the garlic in half and squeeze the soft cloves into a small bowl. Mash the garlic with a fork, then add the extra-virgin olive oil and vinegar. Season with a little salt, white pepper, and a pinch of sugar. If the sauce is quite thick, add 2 tablespoons of hot water to thin it down.

Meanwhile, brush the mushrooms with the light olive oil and bake them for 20 minutes or until they are just beginning to soften.

Slice half of the mushrooms. Put in a bowl with the pine nuts, parsley, and the whole mushrooms. Add the garlic sauce and lightly toss the salad. Top with the Parmesan cheese and serve with thinly sliced and toasted sourdough bread.

white bean and tomato salad

serves 4

2 tablespoons olive oil
2 garlic cloves, crushed
1 red onion, cut into wedges
2 large handfuls thyme sprigs
3 tablespoons white wine
2 cups canned cannellini beans
12 cherry tomatoes, halved
1 tablespoon balsamic vinegar
5 handfuls Italian parsley,
   roughly chopped
salt and pepper, to season
extra-virgin olive oil (optional)

Heat the oil in a frying pan over medium heat. Add the garlic. Cook until lightly golden before adding the red onion and thyme sprigs. Continue cooking until the onion is soft and transparent, then pour in the white wine. Simmer until the wine has reduced to almost nothing before mixing in the beans. Stir to combine and then remove the bean mixture from the heat.

Tip the beans into a bowl. Add the tomatoes, vinegar, and parsley, stir to combine, and season to taste. You can also add a little extra-virgin olive oil to give the salad a rich gloss.

chicken and pine nut salad

serves 4

1 egg yolk
1 teaspoon balsamic vinegar
1/2 cup light olive oil
2 anchovies, finely chopped
sea salt and freshly ground black
   pepper, to season
2 chicken breasts (about 14 ounces),
   poached and shredded
1/4 cup salted capers, rinsed
   and drained
1/4 cup pine nuts, toasted
1/4 cup currants
1 large handful Italian parsley,
   roughly chopped
zest of 1 lemon

Place the egg yolk and vinegar in a small bowl and whisk to combine. Slowly add the oil, whisking to form a thick, creamy mayonnaise. Fold the anchovies through the mayonnaise and season with salt and freshly ground black pepper. Set aside.

Place the remaining ingredients in a large bowl and toss together. Fold in the anchovy mayonnaise. Serve the salad in small bowls and season with freshly ground black pepper to taste.

mushrooms baked in vine leaves

serves 4

24 vine leaves in brine
4 large meadow mushrooms, stalks
   removed
12 cherry tomatoes
2 red onions, cut into eight wedges
4 sprigs thyme
4 tablespoons extra-virgin olive oil
crusty bread, to serve
goat cheese, to serve
fresh pesto (see basics), to serve

Preheat the oven to 350°F. Rinse the vine leaves and drain in a colander. Lay out four pieces of parchment paper, each approximately 8 inches square. Lay three large vine leaves at the center of each square, overlapping the leaves to make a base. Sit one of the mushrooms in the middle of each vine leaf, cap side down.

Divide the cherry tomatoes, onions, and thyme between the four mushrooms, piling them up in the cap. Pour the olive oil over and cover the mushrooms with another three vine leaves, tucking the edges under to make a package. Draw in the four corners of each parchment paper square so that they meet, then twist the joined corners to fasten the edges and seal. Place the packages on a baking sheet and bake for 1 1/2 hours.

To serve, remove the parchment paper and the top vine leaves, so the vegetables are sitting on a bed of baked vine leaves. Serve with crusty bread, goat cheese, and pesto.

capriciosa pizza   serves 4

1 3/4 cups canned plum tomatoes
2 tablespoons extra-virgin olive oil,
  plus extra, for drizzling
2 medium pizza bases (see basics)
sea salt, to season
9 ounces sliced fresh baby
  mozzarella cheese (about 20 balls)
4 slices ham
1/2 cup button mushrooms, sliced
1/2 cup sliced marinated artichoke
  hearts
1/2 cup pitted kalamata olives
2 tablespoons grated Parmesan
  cheese

Preheat the oven to 400°F. Drain and thinly slice the tomatoes, then put them in a saucepan with the extra-virgin olive oil. Simmer over medium heat for 5 minutes. Allow to cool. Spread the tomato over the pizza bases. Season with sea salt, drizzle with a little extra-virgin olive oil, and bake for 15 minutes. Remove from the oven and top with the sliced baby mozzarella cheese, ham, mushrooms, artichoke hearts, and olives. Sprinkle with Parmesan cheese and return to the oven for a few minutes until the cheese has melted.

fennel and tomato salad

serves 4

3 fennel bulbs, trimmed
1 tablespoon thyme
2 tablespoons lemon juice
2/3 cup extra-virgin olive oil
4 tomatoes on the vine, stalks intact
1 tablespoon balsamic vinegar
1 teaspoon superfine sugar
3/4 cup shaved Parmesan cheese
1 handful basil leaves
crusty bread, to serve

Preheat the oven to 400°F. Cut the fennel bulbs from top to base into several thick slices. Place on a baking sheet with the thyme, and drizzle with the lemon juice and 4 tablespoons of the extra-virgin olive oil. Cover with foil and put in the oven.

Place the tomatoes on a smaller baking sheet and drizzle with the vinegar and remaining oil. Sprinkle with the sugar, cover with foil, and put in the oven. Bake the tomatoes and fennel for 30 minutes or until the tomatoes begin to burst.

To assemble, layer the tomatoes, fennel, and Parmesan cheese with the basil leaves. Spoon over the cooking liquids and serve with crusty bread.

warm roast beef salad serves 4

4 plum tomatoes, quartered
  lengthwise
salt and freshly ground black pepper,
  to season
a pinch white sugar
1/2 cup olive oil
1 large eggplant, thinly sliced
1-pound piece tenderloin steak
2 large handfuls arugula
1/3 cup pesto (see basics)

Preheat the oven to 350°F. Put the tomatoes on a baking sheet and season them with salt, freshly ground black pepper, and the pinch of sugar. Bake for 20 minutes.

Heat the oil in a frying pan over high heat and fry the eggplant slices until they are lightly browned on both sides. Remove the eggplant and drain on paper towels. Pour away most of the oil and return the pan to the heat. Sear the beef steak in the frying pan. Place on a baking sheet and bake in the oven for 10 minutes (it will be rare at this point, so cook it for an additional 5 minutes if you prefer). Season the beef with salt, cover with foil, and allow to rest for a few minutes. Arrange the tomatoes and eggplant on a bed of arugula. Thinly slice the beef, arrange on the salad leaves, and season well. Finish with a generous spoonful of pesto.

tart provençal

4 large red onions, cut into six wedges
2 tablespoons olive oil
a few thyme sprigs
1 tablespoon balsamic vinegar
1 prebaked 10-inch short-crust
   tart shell (see basics)
3 ripe plum tomatoes, thickly sliced
10 kalamata olives, pitted and torn
salt and freshly ground black pepper,
   to season
extra-virgin olive oil, to drizzle
torn basil leaves
green salad or goat cheese, to serve

Preheat the oven to 350°F. Put the onions in a heavy-based frying pan with the oil and thyme. Sauté over low heat for 20 minutes or until the onion begins to soften and lightly caramelize. Add the balsamic vinegar, stir to combine, and cook for an additional 5 minutes. Remove from the heat.

Spread the onion in the tart shell. Arrange the tomato slices over the onion, then scatter the olives over the sliced tomato. Season with salt and freshly ground black pepper. Cover with foil and bake for 20 minutes. Remove the foil and bake for an additional 15 minutes. Remove from the oven, drizzle with a little extra-virgin olive oil, and add a scattering of torn basil leaves. Serve with a green salad or goat cheese.

roasted squash salad serves 4

2 red bell peppers
1 small winter squash
  (about 1³/₄ pounds), peeled
4 tablespoons olive oil
1 tablespoon finely chopped
  lemongrass
1 tablespoon lemon juice
1 teaspoon sesame oil
1 teaspoon shaved jaggery
  (or brown sugar)
1 teaspoon soy sauce
2 cups baby arugula
freshly ground black pepper,
  to season

Preheat the oven to 350°F. Roast the bell peppers until the skin is blistered or blackened. Put into a bowl, cover with plastic wrap, and set aside.

Chop the squash into eight large pieces. Put on a baking sheet. Rub with half the oil. Bake for 40 minutes or until the squash is cooked through.

Meanwhile, peel and seed the bell peppers. Finely dice the flesh. Put in a bowl with the lemongrass, lemon juice, sesame oil, jaggery, soy sauce, and remaining olive oil. Gently toss to combine.

Serve the baked squash on a bed of arugula. Spoon the bell pepper over the squash mixture. Season with freshly ground black pepper.

roasted bell pepper and green olive salad

serves 6

2 red bell peppers
2 green bell peppers
2 yellow bell peppers
2 garlic cloves, finely chopped
2 large handfuls parsley,
   roughly chopped
10 large basil leaves, roughly chopped
12 green olives, pitted and sliced
3 tablespoons olive oil
1 tablespoon balsamic vinegar
sea salt and freshly ground black
   pepper, to season

Preheat the oven to 400°F. Roast the peppers whole until the skin blisters, then put them in a plastic bag or covered bowl. When cooled, seed and skin the bell peppers, then thinly slice them and put them in a bowl with the garlic, parsley, basil, sliced olives, olive oil, and balsamic vinegar. Gently toss the ingredients to combine. Season with sea salt and freshly ground black pepper.

pissaladière

4 tablespoons olive oil
4–5 large onions, thinly sliced
1 teaspoon finely chopped rosemary
1 teaspoon finely chopped thyme
1 teaspoon superfine sugar
1 quantity pizza dough (see basics)
12 anchovies
16 black olives, pitted
12 basil leaves, to garnish

Preheat the oven to 425°F. Heat a large frying pan over medium heat and add the oil, onions, rosemary, and thyme. Cover and cook over low heat for 20 minutes or until the onions are very soft. Add the sugar and cook for an additional 1 minute before setting aside.

Turn out the risen dough onto a floured surface and punch it down. Divide into four sections and roll out each piece to form a thin oval. Turn the edges over a little to form a slightly thicker crust. Place on a large oiled cookie sheet. Cover the surface of the pizzas with the onions. Tear the anchovies and olives into small pieces and sprinkle over the onions. Bake for 15 minutes. Remove from the oven and garnish with basil leaves.

three bean salad with prosciutto

serves 4

6 slices prosciutto
2 cups green beans
2 cups wax beans
3/4 cup canned lima beans, rinsed
   and drained
2 tablespoons extra-virgin olive oil
2 tablespoons white wine vinegar
5 handfuls Italian parsley,
   roughly chopped
2 tablespoons pine nuts, toasted
sea salt and freshly ground black
   pepper, to season

Bring a large saucepan of water to a boil. Meanwhile, broil or panfry the prosciutto until it is crisp. Then allow to drain on paper towels.

Blanch the green and wax beans in the boiling water for a few minutes or until the green ones begin to turn an emerald green. Drain the beans and refresh under cold running water.

Return the beans to the saucepan with the lima beans and add the olive oil, vinegar, and parsley. Break the prosciutto into small pieces and add to the beans along with the pine nuts. Toss together and season with sea salt and freshly ground black pepper. Pile onto a serving platter.

sardines on toast

serves 4

3 ripe tomatoes, finely diced
1/2 red onion, thinly sliced into rings
2 tablespoons white wine vinegar
2 tablespoons virgin olive oil
1 tablespoon oregano
sea salt and freshly ground black
  pepper, to season
1/2 tablespoon butter
8 or 16 sardine fillets, depending on
  their size (10 1/2 ounces in total)
4 thick slices whole-wheat bread,
  toasted

Put the tomatoes, onion, vinegar, olive oil, and oregano leaves in a bowl. Stir to combine and season with sea salt and freshly ground black pepper.

Heat a nonstick frying pan over high heat and add the butter. Fry the sardine fillets for 1–2 minutes on both sides or until they are opaque and slightly browned. Pile the sardines onto the toast. Top with the tomato salad and any remaining dressing.

black bean salsa with
tortillas

serves 4

2 tablespoons olive oil
1 garlic clove, crushed
1 tablespoon ground cumin
1 red bell pepper, finely diced
1 cup fresh corn kernels
1 cup cooked black beans
2 large handfuls cilantro leaves,
　roughly chopped
1 large handful mint,
　roughly chopped
1 tablespoon pomegranate molasses
salt and pepper, to season
finely chopped chipotle chili, or
　Tabasco sauce
arugula, sour cream, and tortillas,
　to serve

Heat the olive oil in a frying pan over medium heat and add the garlic, ground cumin, and diced bell pepper. Sauté until the peppers are soft and add the corn and black beans. Cook for an additional 5 minutes or until the corn is golden and soft.

Remove the corn and bean mixture from the heat and tip into a serving bowl. Add the herbs and pomegranate molasses. Season to taste with salt, pepper, and the chipotle chili or Tabasco sauce. Serve with arugula, sour cream, and warm tortillas, or as a side dish to spicy broiled chicken.

marinated seared shrimp with bruschetta

serves 4

4 garlic cloves
1 tablespoon grated fresh ginger
1 large red chili, seeded
1/2 teaspoon ground white pepper
1 tablespoon sesame oil
1/2 cup olive oil
1 lemon, juiced
16 large raw shrimp, peeled and deveined with tails intact
4 thin slices sourdough bread, cut diagonally
1 cup baby spinach leaves
2 scallions, thinly sliced

Put the garlic, ginger, chili, white pepper, sesame oil, olive oil, and lemon juice into a food processor and blend until combined. In a bowl, add the marinade to the shrimp. Toss until the shrimp are well coated. Cover and place in the refrigerator for 1 hour.

Toast the sourdough and put on separate serving plates. Pile with the spinach and scallions.

Sear the shrimp in a frying pan over high heat for 2–3 minutes or until they are pink and starting to curl. Divide the shrimp among the four plates. Pour the remaining marinade into the pan and warm over medium heat. Spoon the hot garlicky oil over the shrimp and serve immediately.

chili corn cakes   serves 4 to 6

1 3/4 cups canned creamed corn
1 cup fine semolina
3/4 cup grated mozzarella cheese
1 cup crumbled goat cheese
4 tablespoons finely chopped cilantro
   leaves
1 teaspoon baking powder
3 jalapeño chilies, finely chopped
2 eggs
sea salt and freshly ground black
   pepper, to season
1/2 cup vegetable oil
6 slices bacon
4 handfuls baby spinach leaves

In a small bowl, mix the creamed corn, semolina, mozzarella, goat cheese, cilantro, baking powder, chilies, and eggs together. Season with sea salt and freshly ground black pepper.

Heat a lightly oiled nonstick frying pan over medium heat and cook the bacon until crisp. Remove and keep warm until ready to serve. Add 2 tablespoons of vegetable oil to the pan. Add 2 heaping tablespoons of batter to form a round corn cake. Cook for 3 minutes on each side or until golden and crusty. Remove and continue with the remaining batter, adding more oil when needed. Serve warm with the bacon and baby spinach leaves.

summer salad with spiced goat cheese

serves 4

1/2 cup fresh goat cheese or light
  goat cheese
1 teaspoon ground cumin
freshly ground black pepper, to season
milk (optional)
1 cup green beans, trimmed
4 plum tomatoes
2 short cucumbers
sea salt, to season
10 mint leaves
2 scallions, thinly sliced
1 handful Italian parsley
4 tablespoons extra-virgin olive oil
1 tablespoon lemon juice

Put the goat cheese into a bowl with the cumin and a grind of black pepper. Stir together to form a soft, thick cream. Add a little milk to the mixture, if needed, to make it softer and easier to stir.

Blanch the green beans in boiling salted water. When they turn bright green, drain and rinse under running cold water. Cut the beans into thin diagonal strips and put in a large bowl. Thickly dice the tomatoes and cucumbers and add them to the beans. Season with a little sea salt, then add the mint, scallions, parsley, extra-virgin olive oil, and lemon juice. Toss together and divide among four plates. Top with a spoonful of the spiced goat cheese.

broiled polenta with mushrooms

serves 4

1/4 cup dried porcini mushrooms

11/2 tablespoons butter

1 garlic clove, finely chopped

11/2 cups cremini mushrooms, thinly sliced

2 cups fresh shiitake mushrooms, thinly sliced

2 cups oyster mushrooms

sea salt and freshly cracked black pepper, to season

1 quantity polenta (see basics)

3 cups arugula, stalks removed

2 tablespoons extra-virgin olive oil

Put the porcini mushrooms in a small bowl. Cover with 1 cup of warm water and soak for 10 minutes. Squeeze any excess liquid from the porcini mushrooms, reserving their soaking liquid, and thinly slice. Put into a deep frying pan with the butter and garlic. Cook over low heat until the garlic is golden. Add the reserved soaking liquid from the porcini and then the cremini and shiitake mushrooms. Cover and simmer for 10 minutes. If the mixture becomes a little dry, add some more water to give the mushrooms a wet texture. At the end of the cooking time, add the whole oyster mushrooms and cook for an additional 3 minutes. Season with sea salt and freshly cracked black pepper.

With a sharp knife, mark out the polenta into large triangles. Cook the polenta under a broiler until the top is golden brown. Pile the warm polenta triangles onto a bed of arugula leaves on four warmed plates. Top with the mushrooms. Drizzle with a little extra-virgin olive oil.

jeweled gazpacho   serves 4

4 short cucumbers
8 ripe tomatoes, roughly chopped
1 tablespoon sea salt
1 teaspoon ground roasted cumin
  seeds
1 small beet, peeled and chopped
1 red bell pepper, diced
3 scallions, thinly sliced
1/2 red onion, finely diced
2 tablespoons chopped cilantro
  leaves
salt and pepper, to season
extra-virgin olive oil, to drizzle

Roughly chop two of the cucumbers and finely dice the remaining two. Put the tomatoes and chopped cucumber into a large bowl with the sea salt and the ground cumin seeds. Stir well and leave to marinate for 2 hours. Put the tomato and cucumber mixture into a blender or food processor with the beet and puree.

Pour the puree into a cheesecloth-lined strainer over a bowl, twist the cheesecloth into a ball, and squeeze out all the liquid. Discard the pulp and chill the juice. When the juice is cold, add the bell pepper, scallions, onion, and cilantro. Chill the gazpacho for an additional 1 hour. Season to taste, ladle into individual bowls, and serve with a drizzle of extra-virgin olive oil.

prosciutto and snap pea salad

serves 4

3 tablespoons olive oil
8 slices prosciutto
2 fennel bulbs, finely shaved
2²/3 cups snap peas, blanched and
    sliced diagonally
10 mint leaves, torn
1 lemon, juiced

Heat the olive oil in a large frying pan over medium heat and fry the prosciutto until just crisp. Set aside to drain on paper towels. Put the fennel, peas, and mint into a bowl. Drizzle with the oil from the pan and the lemon juice. Break the prosciutto into small pieces and add to the salad. Gently toss together and divide among four plates.

tapenade linguine serves 4

5 handfuls Italian parsley,
  roughly chopped
1/4 cup pitted and chopped black olives
1 lemon, zested
4–6 anchovies, finely chopped
1 tablespoon salted capers, rinsed
  and drained
13/4 cup shaved Parmesan cheese
3 tablespoons extra-virgin olive oil
14 ounces linguine

To make the tapenade, put the parsley, olives, lemon zest, anchovies, capers, Parmesan, and olive oil into a large bowl and toss them together.

Cook the pasta in boiling water until al dente, then drain and return to the saucepan. Add the tapenade, toss it through the cooked linguine, and divide among four pasta bowls.

niçoise salad

8 small potatoes
1 1/2 cups green beans
4 eggs
2 small heads butter lettuce
3/4 cup canned Italian-style tuna, or
    white albacore tuna packed in oil,
    drained
2 ripe tomatoes, cut into chunks
1/2 red onion, thinly sliced
20 kalamata olives
1 handful Italian parsley
2 tablespoons salted capers, rinsed
    and drained
8 anchovies

dressing
2 tablespoons lemon juice
4 tablespoons extra-virgin olive oil
1/4 teaspoon crushed garlic

Boil the potatoes until cooked through, then drain and cut in half. Blanch the green beans in boiling water until emerald green, then drain and rinse. Boil the eggs for 6 minutes.

Divide the butter lettuce leaves among four bowls. Shell the eggs and cut in half. Divide the potatoes, beans, and eggs among the bowls. Add the tuna to the bowls, along with the tomatoes and red onion. Add the olives to each bowl, with a light sprinkling of parsley and salted capers.

To make the dressing, combine the lemon juice, olive oil, and garlic. Drizzle the dressing over the salads and then top each salad with the anchovies.

fresh fig and prosciutto pizza

serves 4

1 quantity pizza dough (see basics)
4 1/4 ounces Taleggio cheese,
   thinly sliced
4 fresh figs, thinly sliced
4 slices prosciutto, halved
olive oil, to drizzle
salt and freshly ground black pepper,
   to season
1 handful baby arugula leaves,
   to serve

Preheat the oven to 400°F. Roll out four small circles of the pizza dough, each one 4 1/2 inches in diameter. Put onto a baking sheet and top with the sliced Taleggio, figs, and prosciutto. Drizzle with a little olive oil and season with salt and freshly ground black pepper. Bake for 15 minutes or until the dough is golden brown. Serve with a scattering of arugula leaves.

roasted red bell pepper soup with minted yogurt
seared tuna with olive butter and warm red salad
chili corn and black bean soup warm vegetables with
white beans lasagna with chili crab chili mussels
fish, clam, and herb soup lamb shanks with parsnip,
lemon, and herbs swordfish with prosciutto osso bucco
seaside orzo linguine with shrimp and fresh herbs
vine leaf chicken lamb chops with mint salsa roasted

03   main   meals

tuna with fennel and tomato salsa snapper sausage and
bean stew tomato risotto mussels with rouille orzo
with sweet and sour bell pepper pancetta and pea
risotto tuna with tomato and olives steak with onion
salsa beefsteak with an onion and mushroom sauce

roasted bell pepper soup with minted yogurt

serves 4

4 red bell peppers
4 vine-ripened tomatoes, stems
    removed
1 tablespoon olive oil
3 cups vegetable stock (see basics)
1 teaspoon finely chopped canned
    chipotle chili
1 teaspoon ground cumin
sea salt and freshly ground black
    pepper, to season
1/3 cup plain yogurt
1 tablespoon finely chopped mint

Preheat the oven to 400°F. Put the bell peppers and tomatoes onto a baking sheet and rub with the olive oil. Bake for 30 minutes or until both the bell peppers and tomatoes are slightly blackened and blistered. Remove and allow to cool.

Remove the skins and seeds from the bell peppers and then put into a food processor with the tomatoes. Process into a smooth puree and put in a saucepan with the stock, chili, and cumin. Bring to a boil and then reduce the heat to low. Gently simmer the soup for 10 minutes and season to taste with sea salt and freshly ground black pepper.

In a bowl, combine the yogurt and mint. Ladle the soup into warmed bowls and add a spoonful of the minted yogurt.

pancetta and pea risotto

serves 4

4 cups chicken stock (see basics)
3 tablespoons butter
1 onion, finely diced
8 slices pancetta, finely chopped
4 sage leaves, thinly sliced
1 cup risotto rice
1 cup frozen peas
3/4 cup grated Parmesan cheese
1 small handful Italian parsley
olive oil, to drizzle

Boil the chicken stock in a saucepan. Heat the butter in a large heavy-based saucepan over medium heat and add the onion, pancetta, and sage. Sauté until the onion is soft and transparent. Add the risotto rice. Stir for 1 minute or until the grains are well coated and glossy. Add 1 cup of stock. Simmer and stir until absorbed. Add another 1 cup of stock and stir until absorbed. Add the frozen peas and 1 cup of stock, stirring until absorbed. Test if the rice is al dente. If not fully cooked, add the remaining stock and simmer until the stock has reduced and the rice is coated in a creamy sauce.

Fold the cheese and parsley through the risotto. Spoon into warmed bowls. Serve with a drizzle of olive oil.

seared tuna with olive butter and warm red salad

serves 4

1 red bell pepper
4 ripe tomatoes, quartered
1 red onion, cut into eight wedges
2 tablespoons extra-virgin olive oil
sea salt and freshly ground black
    pepper, to season
3 tablespoons butter, softened
6 black olives, pitted and finely
    chopped
2 tablespoons finely chopped
    Italian parsley
four 5^{1}/$_{2}$-ounce tuna fillets

Preheat the oven to 350°F. Slice the bell pepper into thick strips and place on a baking sheet. Add the tomatoes and red onion, drizzle with the extra-virgin olive oil and season with sea salt and freshly ground black pepper. Cover the vegetables with foil and bake for 30 minutes.

Combine the butter, chopped olives, and parsley in a small bowl.

Sear the tuna fillets in a frying pan for 2–3 minutes on both sides. Serve with the warm red salad and a dollop of the olive butter.

fresh lasagna with chili crab

4 tablespoons olive oil
2 large red chilies, seeded and
  thinly sliced
1/2 teaspoon smoked paprika
2 garlic cloves, crushed
3 leeks, thinly sliced
13/4 cups canned chopped tomatoes
1 teaspoon superfine sugar
1/2 cup white wine
sea salt and freshly ground black
  pepper, to season
1 cup crabmeat
8 fresh lasagna sheets
11/2 cups baby spinach leaves
1/4 cup chives, cut into 11/4-inch
  lengths

Bring a large saucepan of salted water to a boil. Heat the olive oil in a large pan over medium heat and add the chilies, paprika, and garlic. Cook for 1 minute before adding the leeks. Cover and simmer for 5 minutes or until the leeks are soft. Add the tomatoes, 3/4 cup water, the sugar, and the wine. Simmer for an additional 10 minutes. Season with sea salt and freshly ground black pepper.

Put the crabmeat into a bowl and break up into fine threads with a fork. Add the crabmeat to the tomato sauce.

Cook the lasagna in the boiling water until al dente. Drain the lasagna and put one sheet on a warmed plate. Spoon a little sauce onto half the sheet, add the spinach, then fold over. Repeat with the remaining ingredients.

Serve with a sprinkling of chives.

Parmesan lamb pies   serves 4

2 tablespoons olive oil
2 onions, peeled and finely diced
2 garlic cloves, chopped
18 ounces ground lamb
2 celery stalks, finely chopped
1/4 cup grated carrot
1 teaspoon ground cinnamon
13/4 cups canned chopped tomatoes
1 cup red wine
sea salt and freshly ground black
   pepper, to season
3 eggs
1/3 cup yogurt
1 cup grated Parmesan cheese

Preheat the oven to 400°F. Heat the olive oil in a frying pan over medium heat, then add the onions and garlic. Cook until the onion begins to soften and turn a golden brown. Add the lamb and increase the heat. Brown the lamb and then add the celery, carrot, cinnamon, tomatoes, and wine. Reduce the heat to medium and simmer until the liquid has reduced. Season to taste with sea salt and freshly ground black pepper.

Spoon the mixture into four individual ramekins or a medium baking dish. Put the eggs, yogurt, and half the Parmesan into a bowl and whisk to combine. Spoon the mixture over the pies and sprinkle with the remaining Parmesan. Bake for 20 minutes or until the top is golden brown.

chili, corn, and black bean soup

serves 4

6 corncobs
1 tablespoon olive oil
2 red onions, diced
2 garlic cloves, very finely chopped
1 red chili, seeded and finely chopped
2 tablespoons tomato paste
1 teaspoon smoked paprika
4 cups chicken or vegetable stock
   (see basics)
1 cup cooked black beans
1/3 cup sour cream
extra paprika and cilantro leaves,
   to serve

With a sharp knife, slice away the kernels from the corncobs and set aside.

Put a large saucepan over medium heat and add the olive oil, onions, garlic, and chili. Cook for 5 minutes or until the onion is transparent and soft. Add the corn kernels, tomato paste, paprika, and stock. Bring to a boil. Reduce the heat to a simmer and cook for 15 minutes. Add the cooked black beans just before serving, then garnish the soup with the sour cream, extra paprika, and cilantro leaves.

pappardelle with basil, feta, and bell pepper serves 4

4 red bell peppers
3 tablespoons extra-virgin olive oil
1 teaspoon balsamic vinegar
1 large handful basil
salt and pepper, to season
14 ounces pappardelle pasta
1 cup feta cheese

Preheat the oven to 400°F. Rub the bell peppers with 2 tablespoons of the oil, slice them in half lengthwise, and put them on a baking sheet with the skin facing up. Bake for about 20 minutes or until the skin blackens and blisters. Place the bell peppers in a plastic bag or bowl covered in plastic wrap. Allow them to cool and then remove the skin and seeds. Put the flesh of the peppers into a blender with the balsamic vinegar and 10 basil leaves. Season and blend. Add the strained liquid from the baking sheet and the remaining 1 tablespoon of oil to give the bell peppers a saucelike consistency. Heat the sauce in a large saucepan over low heat to keep it warm while you cook the pasta.

Cook the pappardelle in a saucepan of boiling water until it is al dente, then drain the pasta and add it to the sauce. Crumble half the feta through the pasta and toss. Serve garnished with basil leaves and the remaining feta cheese crumbled on top.

vine leaf chicken   serves 4

2 cups cherry tomatoes
1 handful mint
1 handful Italian parsley
1 cup firm ricotta cheese
1 egg
four 7-ounce boneless, skinless
  chicken breasts
12 whole vine leaves in brine
sea salt and freshly ground black
  pepper, to season
1 cup white wine
1 lemon, juiced
2 handfuls mixed baby leaf salad
2 tablespoons extra-virgin olive oil

Preheat the oven to 400°F. Puree the tomatoes, 8 large mint leaves, and the parsley in a food processor. Stir in the ricotta cheese and the egg and set aside. Pound the chicken pieces until they are 1/4-inch thick. Put each chicken piece onto three overlapping vine leaves and spread the ricotta cheese mixture over the surface of each one. Season with a little sea salt and freshly ground black pepper. Roll up and secure each wrap with a toothpick. Arrange the wraps in a baking dish. Pour the white wine and lemon juice over and cover with foil. Bake for 30 minutes. Remove and allow to cool.

Unwrap the vine leaves and lay a vine leaf on a serving plate. Top with some baby leaf salad. Slice the chicken and arrange on top of the salad with the remaining mint leaves. Drizzle with the extra-virgin olive oil.

tomato and basil soup serves 4

3 tablespoons olive oil
2 red onions, thinly sliced
2 garlic cloves, finely chopped
8 roughly chopped ripe tomatoes
4 cups vegetable stock (see basics)
15 large basil leaves
1 tablespoon soy sauce
sea salt and freshly ground black
   pepper, to season

Heat the olive oil, onions, and garlic in a large saucepan over medium heat. Sauté until the onion is transparent, then add the tomatoes and cook for 5 minutes. Add the vegetable stock. Bring almost to a boil, then reduce the heat and simmer for 20 minutes. Remove from the heat and allow to cool. Add the basil and soy sauce. Transfer to a blender and mix until smooth. Return the soup to the saucepan, season to taste with sea salt and freshly ground black pepper, and heat to serve.

fettuccine with chili, corn, and shrimp

serves 4

2 tablespoons olive oil
2 small red chilies, seeded and
   finely chopped
1 teaspoon smoked paprika
3 scallions, thinly sliced
3 corncobs, kernels removed
3 vine-ripened tomatoes, finely
   chopped
20 raw medium shrimp, peeled and
   deveined with tails intact
sea salt and freshly ground black
   pepper, to season
14 ounces fettuccine
2 handfuls baby arugula leaves
2 tablespoons extra-virgin olive oil

Bring a large saucepan of salted water to a boil.

Heat the olive oil in a large frying pan over medium heat and add the chilies, paprika, and scallions. Stir-fry for 1 minute, then add the corn and tomatoes. Cook for a few minutes or until the corn is soft and a deep golden color. Add the shrimp and continue to cook for 2–3 minutes or until the shrimp are pink and have curled up. Remove from the heat and season to taste with sea salt and freshly ground black pepper.

Add the fettuccine to the boiling water and cook until al dente. Drain and return to the saucepan. Pour in the corn and shrimp sauce, add the arugula leaves, and stir through. Divide among four bowls and drizzle with the extra-virgin olive oil.

warm vegetables with white beans

1/2 cup olive oil

6 slices pancetta, finely chopped

1 red onion, finely diced

2 garlic cloves, crushed

1 teaspoon finely chopped rosemary
leaves

2 celery stalks, thinly sliced

1 large eggplant, finely diced

2 red bell peppers, finely diced

1 3/4 cups canned chopped tomatoes

1 orange, zest grated, juiced

1 3/4 cups canned cannellini beans,
drained and rinsed

2 tablespoons roughly chopped
Italian parsley

2 tablespoons extra-virgin olive oil

basil leaves, to serve

crusty bread, to serve

Heat the oil in a large frying pan over medium heat and add the pancetta, onion, garlic, and rosemary. Cook until the onion begins to soften and then add the celery, eggplant, and bell peppers. When the eggplant begins to soften, add the chopped tomatoes, orange zest, and orange juice. Cover and continue to cook over low heat for 30 minutes. Add the cannellini beans and cook for an additional 1–2 minutes, then fold in the parsley and spoon into a serving dish. Drizzle with the extra-virgin olive oil and sprinkle with basil leaves. Serve with warm crusty bread or as a side dish to roasted lamb.

fisherman's soup   serves 4

2 tablespoons olive oil
1 onion, thinly sliced
2 garlic cloves, crushed
pinch saffron threads
1 fennel bulb, finely diced
3 ripe tomatoes, finely chopped
6 cups fish stock (see basics)
18 ounces cod fillets, cut into
   bite-size pieces
sea salt and freshly ground black
   pepper, to season
lemon, to serve
extra-virgin olive oil, to serve
crusty bread, to serve

Heat the olive oil in a large saucepan and add the onion, garlic, and saffron. Cook over low to medium heat until the onion is soft but not brown. Add the fennel and cook for a couple of minutes before adding the tomatoes. Add the fish stock and simmer for 10 minutes. Add the cod fillet pieces and simmer for an additional few minutes or until the fish is cooked through. Season to taste with sea salt and freshly ground black pepper and serve with some lemon, a drizzle of extra-virgin olive oil, and warm crusty bread.

orzo with sweet and sour bell pepper

serves 6

1 red onion, thinly sliced
2 red bell peppers, thickly sliced
2 tablespoons balsamic vinegar
2 tablespoons soft brown sugar
sea salt and black pepper, to season
1¼ cups orzo
2 large ripe tomatoes, roughly chopped
10 large basil leaves, roughly torn
2 handfuls baby arugula leaves
4 tablespoons extra-virgin olive oil

Preheat the oven to 350°F. Put the onion, bell pepper, vinegar, and sugar in an ovenproof dish and toss them together. Season the vegetables with a little sea salt, cover with foil, and bake for 30 minutes.

Remove the baking dish and allow the vegetables to cool. Cook the orzo in a large saucepan of rapidly boiling water for 10 minutes or until al dente, then drain it well.

Put the orzo in a large bowl with the bell pepper mixture, tomatoes, basil, and arugula leaves and toss to combine. Season to taste and drizzle with the extra-virgin olive oil.

shrimp with fresh tomato sauce

serves 4

2 tablespoons olive oil

5 garlic cloves, thinly sliced

5 scallions, peeled and thinly sliced

5 Kaffir lime leaves

5 vine-ripened tomatoes, finely chopped

1 1/2 tablespoons jaggery, shaved (or brown sugar)

4 tablespoons lime juice

1 tablespoon fish sauce

20 raw jumbo shrimp, peeled and deveined with tails intact

To make the tomato sauce, heat the oil in a saucepan over medium heat and cook the garlic and scallions until golden brown. Add the Kaffir lime leaves and tomatoes and simmer for 5 minutes or until the tomatoes are soft. Add the jaggery, lime juice, and fish sauce and gently simmer for an additional 10 minutes. Remove from the heat.

Heat a nonstick frying pan over high heat and sear the shrimp for 2–3 minutes or until pink on both sides and beginning to curl up. Serve with the tomato sauce.

tomato risotto

serves 4

4 cups chicken stock (see basics)
3 tablespoons butter
1 tablespoon olive oil, plus extra to
   drizzle
1 red onion, diced
1 cup risotto rice
1/2 cup white wine
8 ripe tomatoes, halved, seeds
   removed, cut into bite-size chunks
1 cup grated Parmesan cheese
basil leaves, to serve

Heat the chicken stock in a saucepan.

Heat the butter and olive oil in a large heavy-based saucepan over medium heat. Add the onion and sauté until soft and transparent. Add the risotto rice and stir for 1 minute or until the grains are coated and glossy. Add the white wine. Simmer and stir until absorbed. Add 1 cup of stock and stir until absorbed. Add the tomatoes and 1 cup of stock and stir until the stock is absorbed. Stir in another 1 cup of stock. When absorbed, test if the rice is al dente. If undercooked, add the remaining stock and simmer until the stock has reduced and the rice is coated in a creamy sauce.

Fold the Parmesan cheese through, then put into bowls. Serve with a drizzle of olive oil and a sprinkling of basil leaves.

fish, clam, and herb soup

serves 4

18 ounces live clams in the shell
4 tablespoons olive oil
2 onions, finely chopped
2 garlic cloves, crushed
1/2 teaspoon thyme
1/2 teaspoon smoked paprika
14 sage leaves, 2 finely chopped
1/2 teaspoon finely chopped rosemary
1/2 cup white wine
4 large ripe tomatoes, finely diced
2 large potatoes, finely diced
2 tablespoons tomato paste
18 ounces whitefish fillets, cut into
  bite-size pieces
3 tablespoons finely chopped
  Italian parsley

Soak the clams in water for about 10 minutes, discarding any that don't close when tapped.

Heat half the oil in a saucepan over medium heat. Add the onions, garlic, thyme, paprika, chopped sage, and rosemary. Cook until the onions are transparent, then add the wine and clams. Cover and cook for 1 minute. When the clams have opened, lift them out and set aside. Add the tomatoes, potatoes, tomato paste, and 3 cups of water. Simmer for 10 minutes, then add the fish and cook for another 5 minutes.

Meanwhile, fry the whole sage leaves in the remaining oil until crispy. Add the parsley and clams to the soup, then garnish with the crisp sage leaves.

steak with onion salsa serves 4

2 large red onions, thickly sliced
2 ripe tomatoes
2 handfuls Italian parsley
10 oregano leaves
1 tablespoon balsamic vinegar
3 tablespoons extra-virgin olive oil
sea salt and freshly ground black
    pepper, to season
four 6-ounce tenderloin steaks

Preheat a barbecue hotplate or charbroil pan to high heat. To make the onion salsa, broil the onion until it is quite blackened on both sides. Remove and put on a cutting board. Put the tomatoes on the barbecue. Roughly chop the cooked onion and transfer to a bowl. Once the tomatoes begin to blacken, turn over and cook for 1 minute more. Put them in the bowl with the onions and roughly chop with a sharp knife or a pair of kitchen scissors. Add the parsley, oregano, balsamic vinegar, and extra-virgin olive oil. Season with sea salt and freshly ground black pepper to taste and toss the salsa ingredients together.

Meanwhile, put the steaks on the barbecue and sear for 2–3 minutes. Turn over and cook for an additional 1 minute. Remove from the barbecue and set aside to rest. Serve with the onion salsa.

tuna with tomato and olives

serves 4

20 cherry tomatoes, quartered
20 basil leaves
32 small black olives
2 tablespoons balsamic vinegar
4 tablespoons extra-virgin olive oil
2 teaspoons olive oil
four 7-ounce tuna steaks
green leaf salad, to serve

Put the tomatoes, basil leaves, olives, balsamic vinegar, and extra-virgin olive oil into a bowl and mix.

Heat the olive oil in a frying pan over high heat. Add the tuna steaks and sear them on one side for 1 minute. Turn the tuna steaks over, reduce the heat to medium, and cook them for an additional 3–4 minutes.

Put the tuna onto warmed plates and top with the tomatoes and olives. Serve with a green leaf salad.

chili mussels

4 1/2 pounds black mussels
3 tablespoons olive oil
1 teaspoon red chili flakes
3 garlic cloves, finely chopped
15 saffron threads
4 1/2 cups canned peeled tomatoes
1/4 cup tomato paste
3/4 cup white wine
1 large handful Italian parsley,
   roughly chopped
crusty bread, to serve

Clean the mussels under cold running water, scrubbing them to remove any barnacles or bits of hairy "beard." Discard any that are open and that do not close when you tap them.

Heat the olive oil in a large saucepan over medium heat and sauté the chili, garlic, and saffron for 1 minute. Add the tomatoes, breaking them up as you stir. Mix in the tomato paste and cook for 10 minutes. Bring to a boil and add the mussels. Cover and cook for 3 minutes or until they have all opened, discarding any that haven't. Reduce the heat to a simmer and remove the mussels to four warmed bowls. Add the white wine to the pan and cook for another 2 minutes before ladling the hot broth over the mussels. Garnish with the parsley and serve with warm crusty bread.

lamb chops with mint salsa

serves 4

1 short cucumber, finely diced
2 tablespoons finely diced red onion
2 tablespoons balsamic vinegar
1 tablespoon extra-virgin olive oil
3 handfuls mint
1 tablespoon superfine sugar
1 tablespoon vegetable oil
12 small lamb chops
salt and pepper, to season
roasted sweet potatoes (see basics)

To make the salsa, put the cucumber, red onion, vinegar, and olive oil in a small bowl and toss them together. Finely chop the mint leaves, sprinkling them with sugar halfway through the chopping. Add the mint and sugar to the bowl and stir them into the salsa.

Heat the oil in a frying pan and sear the lamb chops on one side until golden brown. Turn over and cook the other side for another 2–4 minutes, depending on how thick the chops are. Remove the pan from the heat, season the chops, and allow to rest.

Divide among four plates and add some salsa to each chop. Serve with roasted sweet potatoes.

seared tuna with red bell peppers and anchovies

2 tablespoons vegetable oil
2 red bell peppers
4 anchovies, roughly chopped
1 handful Italian parsley
12 basil leaves
4 tablespoons extra-virgin olive oil
freshely ground black pepper, to
    season
four 5 1/2-ounce tuna steaks
2 handfuls baby spinach leaves
1 tablespoon balsamic vinegar

Heat half the vegetable oil in a frying pan over high heat. Add the bell peppers and sear, turning until they are blistered on all sides. Transfer to a bowl and cover with plastic wrap. When the bell peppers are cool, remove the seeds, stalk, and any skin that rubs off easily, making sure you catch the liquid in the bowl.

Slice the bell peppers into thin strips and put into another bowl. Strain the liquid from the first bowl over them. Add the anchovies, parsley, basil, and extra-virgin olive oil. Season with freshly ground black pepper. Heat the remaining vegetable oil in the frying pan over high heat. Add the tuna and sear on one side for 1 minute. Turn the tuna steaks over, reduce the heat to medium, and cook for 3–4 minutes. Divide the spinach among four plates, top with the tuna, and spoon over the bell pepper salad. Drizzle with the balsamic vinegar and serve.

mussels with rouille serves 4

4 1/2 pounds mussels
2 tablespoons olive oil
1 onion, finely chopped
2 garlic cloves, crushed
3 large ripe tomatoes, diced
1 bay leaf
1 fennel bulb, thinly sliced
1 pinch saffron threads
1 teaspoon sea salt
1 cup white wine
1 large handful Italian parsley
1 quantity rouille (see basics)
crusty white bread, to serve

Clean the mussels under cold running water, scrubbing them to remove any barnacles or bits of hairy "beard." Discard any that are open and that do not close when you tap them.

Put the oil, onion, and garlic into a saucepan and cook over low heat until the onion is transparent. Add the tomatoes, bay leaf, fennel, and saffron. Season with the sea salt and simmer for 10 minutes. Pour in the white wine, bring the sauce to a boil, and add the mussels. Cover with the lid and cook for a few minutes, shaking the pan once or twice. Check that all the mussels have opened. Discard any that remain closed.

Divide the mussels among four bowls, sprinkle with the parsley, and serve with the rouille and crusty white bread.

lamb shanks with parsnip, lemon, and herbs

serves 4

4 red onions, quartered
6 garlic cloves, thinly sliced
4 sprigs thyme
4 lamb shanks (about 2¾ pounds)
1 large parsnip, peeled
8 sage leaves
salt and pepper, to season
1 cup veal stock (see basics)

gremolata
1 tablespoon small capers, rinsed
  and drained
1 garlic clove, crushed
1 lemon, zested
3 handfuls Italian parsley

Preheat the oven to 400°F. Make a bed of the onions, garlic, and thyme in a deep casserole dish. Put the shanks on top, then arrange the parsnip and sage leaves over them and season well. Pour the veal stock over and cover with a lid or foil. Bake for 1 hour, then uncover and bake for an additional 30 minutes or until the meat is pulling away from the bones.

To make the gremolata, place the capers, garlic, lemon zest, and parsley on a chopping board and chop them together finely. Serve sprinkled over the lamb shanks.

roasted tuna with fennel and tomato

serves 4

4 ripe tomatoes

2 garlic cloves, thinly sliced

14–16 sprigs thyme

1/2 cup small black olives

18-ounce tuna fillet

2 tablespoons freshly ground black pepper

1/2 cup olive oil

sea salt, to season

15 basil leaves, roughly torn

1 fennel bulb, sliced paper thin

2 tablespoons extra-virgin olive oil

Preheat the oven to 400°F. Bring a saucepan of salted water to a boil. Make a small X-shaped incision at the base of each tomato and put in the boiling water for 1 minute. Remove with a slotted spoon and put in a bowl to cool.

Lay the garlic and thyme over the base of a deep roasting pan. Sprinkle with the olives. Roll the tuna fillet in the black pepper. Place in the pan, drizzle with the olive oil, and season with sea salt. Seal the roasting pan with foil and bake for 25 minutes.

Peel the tomatoes and put in a bowl. Using a sharp knife, chop into bite-size pieces. Season with sea salt. Add the basil leaves and toss through. Remove the tuna from the oven and slice thinly. Remove the olives from the roasting pan and add to the tomato mixture along with 1–2 tablespoons of the cooking liquid.

On a plate, layer the fennel with the tomato. Top with several slices of tuna. Drizzle with olive oil and garnish with thyme from the roasting pan.

roast beef

4¹/2 **pounds rib joint of beef**
olive oil
1 teaspoon sea salt
1 teaspoon freshly ground black pepper

Preheat the oven to 425°F. Stand the beef in a roasting pan and allow to warm to room temperature. Rub the beef all over with olive oil and season with sea salt and freshly ground black pepper. Roast for 20 minutes, then reduce the heat to 350°F and roast for an additional 1 hour.

Transfer the beef to a warm serving platter, cover it with aluminium foil, and allow to rest for 15 minutes before carving. Serve with roasted vegetables, mustard, horseradish, and Yorkshire puddings.

swordfish with prosciutto

serves 4

8 kalamata olives, pitted
4 1/2 tablespoons butter, softened
2 tablespoons light olive oil
4 slices prosciutto
8 small fingerling or salad potatoes,
   thinly sliced
6 scallions, trimmed and sliced
   diagonally
1 1/2 cups white wine
four 7-ounce swordfish steaks
green salad or steamed green beans,
   to serve

Finely chop the olives and stir into the butter. Set aside until needed.

Heat the oil in a large frying pan over medium heat. Add the prosciutto and fry until crisp. Once the prosciutto is cooked, move it to one side of the pan and add the potato slices and scallions. When the potatoes begin to soften, add the white wine and the swordfish, arranging the swordfish on top of the potatoes and putting a piece of cooked prosciutto on top of each steak. Cover the pan and simmer for 12 minutes.

Check that the fish steaks are cooked through and then serve the swordfish and potatoes on warmed serving plates. Divide the olive butter among the steaks and spoon the wine sauce over the top. Serve with a green salad or steamed green beans.

lamb chops with couscous salad

serves 4

1/3 cup couscous
1/4 tablespoon butter
2 teaspoons ground cumin
3 ripe plum tomatoes, diced
1 short cucumber, diced
1/2 red onion, finely diced
1 handful Italian parsley,
    roughly chopped
1 tablespoon balsamic vinegar
3 tablespoons extra-virgin olive oil
sea salt and freshly ground black
    pepper, to season
12 lamb chops

Put the couscous in a bowl and add the butter, cumin, and 1/2 cup of boiling water. Cover and allow to soak for 2–3 minutes.

Meanwhile, combine the tomatoes, cucumber, onion, parsley, vinegar, and olive oil in a large bowl. Season with sea salt and freshly ground black pepper and stir until all the ingredients are coated in the dressing. Fluff the couscous with a fork, then toss it through the salad.

Barbecue or broil the lamb chops for 2–3 minutes on each side. Remove from the heat, season with sea salt, and allow to rest for 1 minute. Spoon the couscous salad onto four plates and top with the chops.

chili tomato cod

serves 4

4 tablespoons olive oil
4 green chilies, seeded and finely
  chopped
1 teaspoon paprika
1 tablespoon finely grated fresh ginger
1 red onion, thinly sliced
1 tablespoon soft brown sugar
2 cups cherry tomatoes
four 7-ounce cod fillets or other firm
  whitefish fillets
10 sprigs thyme
3 tablespoons butter
1 handful cilantro leaves
steamed green beans, to serve

Heat the olive oil in a deep heavy-based frying pan over medium heat and add the chilies, paprika, ginger, and red onion. Cook for 5 minutes, then add the brown sugar, 3/4 cup of water, and the tomatoes. Continue to cook for an additional 5 minutes and then add the fish fillets. Cover with the thyme. Simmer for 5 minutes or until the fish is cooked through. Remove the fillets and place them on four warmed serving plates.

Add the butter to the sauce and stir until it has melted into the tomatoes. Spoon the tomato sauce over the fish and garnish with cilantro. Serve with steamed green beans.

sausage and white bean stew

3¹/2 cups canned cannellini beans,
 drained and rinsed
5 ripe plum tomatoes, chopped
1³/4 cups canned chopped tomatoes
2 leeks, roughly chopped
8 garlic cloves, peeled
1 tablespoon thyme
1 cup white wine
4 good-quality thick, spicy sausages
1 large handful Italian parsley,
 roughly chopped
crusty bread, to serve

Preheat the oven to 350°F. Put the beans, all the tomatoes, the leeks, garlic, thyme, and white wine into a casserole or ovenproof dish.

Prick the skins of the sausages with a fork and then sear them in a frying pan over high heat until they are browned on all sides. Cut the sausages into bite-size pieces and put them into the casserole dish. Lightly stir together, then cover the dish with a lid or foil and bake for 1 hour.

Sprinkle with the parsley and serve with warm crusty bread.

ocean trout in tomato and orange marinade
serves 4

four 5¹/2-ounce skinless ocean trout
   fillets, boned
2 tablespoons olive oil
sea salt and freshly ground black
   pepper, to season
1 handful Italian parsley
1 lemon, zested, juiced
1 orange, zested, juiced
4 vine-ripened tomatoes, finely diced
¹/4 cup finely chopped scallions
1 tablespoon small salted capers,
   rinsed and drained
spinach leaves, to serve

Slice the trout fillets into 1¹/2-inch wide slices. Heat half the olive oil in a large, heavy-based frying pan over medium heat and sear the trout for 1 minute on all sides. Place on a serving dish and season with sea salt and freshly ground black pepper.

Sprinkle the parsley over the fish. Add the citrus juice and zest, tomatoes, scallions, and capers to the pan and cook for 1 minute. Pour over the fish and drizzle with the remaining olive oil. Allow to rest for 1 hour.

Serve the trout fillets on a salad of spinach leaves with a spoonful of the marinade.

lamb shanks with white beans

serves 4

1 cup all-purpose flour
4 lamb shanks (about 2³/₄ pounds)
²/₃ cup olive oil
1 large red onion, thinly sliced
2 garlic cloves, crushed
1 teaspoon rosemary
1 celery stalk, diced
2 carrots, thinly sliced into rounds
1 cup dried kidney beans, soaked
    overnight
2 cups veal stock (see basics)
¹/₂ cup dry Marsala
horseradish gremolata (see basics)

Preheat the oven to 400°F. Put the flour in a plastic bag, add the shanks, and toss until well coated.

Heat half the olive oil in a casserole dish. Add the shanks and turn until they are browned on all sides. Remove from the heat and set aside.

Heat the remaining oil in a frying pan over medium heat. Add the onion, garlic, and rosemary and cook until the onion is soft and lightly golden. Spoon the onion, celery, carrots, and soaked beans over the lamb shanks. Then add the stock and Marsala. Cover and cook for 2 hours, moving the shanks around in the liquid halfway through. Serve with a sprinkle of the horseradish gremolata.

swordfish with a pine nut sauce

serves 4

1 slice white bread, crusts removed
heaping 1/3 cup pine nuts
1/2 garlic clove
2 tablespoons lemon juice
1 tablespoon olive oil
four 6-ounce swordfish steaks
salad of tomatoes, red onion, and basil

Soak the bread in cold water and then squeeze it dry. Put the pine nuts, bread, garlic, and lemon juice in a food processor. Process to a smooth paste. Add 1/4 cup water to thin it to a pourable consistency.

Heat the olive oil in a large frying pan over high heat. Sear the swordfish steaks on one side for 2 minutes or until golden brown. Then turn them over and reduce the heat. Cook the other side for an additional 2–3 minutes or until the steaks are cooked through—they should feel firm when pressed.

Spoon the sauce over the fish and serve with a salad of tomatoes, red onion, and basil.

roasted chicken   serves 4

one 4-pound chicken
1 handful lemon thyme
salt, to season
1 white onion, cut into quarters
3 lemons, halved
1 tablespoon chilled butter

Preheat the oven to 400°F. Rinse the chicken under cold running water and pat dry with paper towels. Sprinkle most of the lemon thyme over the base of a roasting pan. Generously rub the chicken skin with salt and put the chicken on top of the herbs, breast-side up.

Put the onion and 1 of the halved lemons inside the chicken cavity along with a few sprigs of lemon thyme. Place your finger under the skin that covers the breast and slightly pull it away from the flesh. Put the butter under the skin. Repeat on the other side.

Bake for 1 hour, 15 minutes or until the chicken is cooked through. To test if the chicken is cooked, pull a leg away from the body—the juices that run out should be clear and not pink. When the chicken is ready, squeeze the remaining 2 lemons over it and bake for an additional 5 minutes. Remove from the oven and allow the chicken to rest for about 10 minutes before carving. Arrange the chicken pieces on a serving platter and pour some of the lemony pan juices over them.

seaside orzo   serves 4

1 cup orzo
3 tablespoons butter
12 saffron threads
2 garlic cloves, crushed
1 3/4 cup canned chopped tomatoes
2 cups white wine
12 raw jumbo shrimp, peeled and
   deveined with tails intact
16 black mussels, cleaned
2 tablespoons finely chopped
   preserved lemon
1 handful Italian parsley

Bring a large saucepan of salted water to a boil. Cook the orzo until it is al dente, then drain and set aside.

In a deep, wide frying pan or wok, heat the butter, saffron, and garlic until the butter begins to bubble. Add the tomatoes and white wine and simmer for 2 minutes. Add the orzo, shrimp, and mussels to the tomato mixture and cover the pan with a lid. Simmer until the mussels have opened, discarding any that don't. Remove from the heat and divide the mixture between four warm pasta bowls. Garnish with preserved lemon and parsley.

sage and parmesan veal chops

serves 4

4 sage leaves
1 cup fresh bread crumbs
1/3 cup grated Parmesan cheese
2 tablespoons roughly chopped
  Italian parsley
1/4 teaspoon sea salt
freshly ground black pepper, to season
2 eggs
four 7-ounce veal chops
3 tablespoons butter
2 tablespoons olive oil
lemon wedges, to serve
green salad, to serve

Preheat the oven to 400°F. Put the sage, bread crumbs, Parmesan, and parsley into a food processor. Season with the sea salt and some freshly ground black pepper. Process until fine bread crumbs form. Beat the eggs in a bowl and set aside.

Dip each chop into the egg mixture, then press firmly into the bread crumbs.

Heat the butter and olive oil in an ovenproof frying pan over medium to high heat. Cook the chops for 2 minutes on each side, then bake for 12 minutes. Serve with lemon wedges and a green salad.

salsa snapper

2 ripe tomatoes, finely chopped

1 short cucumber, finely chopped

1/2 red onion, finely diced

2 large red chilies, seeded and
thinly sliced

1 handful cilantro leaves

2 teaspoons ground cumin

2 teaspoons fish sauce

2 tablespoons lemon juice

4 tablespoons olive oil

sea salt and freshly ground black
pepper, to season

four 7-ounce snapper fillets, skin on

2 tablespoons vegetable oil

Preheat the oven to 350°F. Gently stir the tomatoes, cucumber, onion, chilies, cilantro, cumin, fish sauce, lemon juice, and olive oil together in a small bowl. Season to taste with sea salt and freshly ground black pepper.

Rinse the fish fillets and pat dry with paper towels. Heat the vegetable oil in a large ovenproof frying pan over high heat. Season the fillets liberally with sea salt and put them, skin-side down, in the hot frying pan. Sear the fillets for 1–2 minutes or until the skin is crisp and golden, then turn them over.

Put the fillets in the frying pan in the oven and bake for 8 minutes. Transfer the fillets to a serving dish, cover each with a spoonful of the tomato salsa, and serve immediately.

osso bucco

four 1¹/₂-inch thick slices of veal shank
¹/₃ cup all-purpose flour
1 teaspoon sea salt
4 tablespoons olive oil
1 leek, washed and thinly sliced
1 celery stalk, finely chopped
1³/₄ cups canned chopped tomatoes
1 cup red wine
1 orange, zested and juiced
arugula, to serve
polenta (see basics), to serve

Put the veal shanks, flour, and sea salt into a clean plastic bag and toss until each shank is lightly coated in the flour. Heat the oil in a large stoveproof casserole dish over medium heat and brown the shanks, two at a time, on all sides. Remove and set aside. Add the leek and celery and cook until the leek is soft. Add the tomatoes and cook over high heat for 5 minutes. Add the wine and the orange zest and juice. Stir to combine, then add the shanks. Cover the casserole dish and reduce to a simmer. Cook for 1¹/₂ hours. Serve with arugula and warm polenta.

cod with saffron and capers
serves 4

4 plum tomatoes, thickly diced
1 leek, washed and thinly sliced
10 saffron threads
1 tablespoon salted capers, rinsed
   and drained
1 cup white wine
four 7-ounce cod fillets or other firm
   whitefish fillets
sea salt and freshly ground black
   pepper, to season
1 1/2 tablespoons butter
2 tablespoons small black olives
1 handful Italian parsley
boiled potatoes, to serve

Preheat the oven to 350°F. Put the tomatoes in a stoveproof casserole or roasting pan over medium heat. Top with the leek, then sprinkle with the saffron and capers. Add the wine and bring to a boil. Reduce the heat to a simmer and cook for an additional 10 minutes. Add the fish, then season lightly with sea salt and freshly ground black pepper and dot with the butter. Cover and bake for 15 minutes.

Remove and place the fish on serving plates. Spoon the sauce over, then garnish with the olives and parsley. Serve with boiled potatoes.

beefsteak with an onion and mushroom sauce

serves 4

1/2 cup dried porcini mushrooms

2 red onions, cut into eighths lengthwise

1 cup red wine

1 garlic clove, crushed

1 tablespoon olive oil

four 6-ounce tenderloin steaks

salt pepper, to season

2 cups oyster mushrooms

3 tablespoons butter

cannellini bean and chopped basil salad, to serve

Soak the dried mushrooms in 1 cup of boiling water for 10 minutes, then drain, reserving the liquid.

Put the onions in a large saucepan and add the wine, garlic, and the mushroom soaking liquid. Slice the soaked mushrooms thinly and add them to the saucepan. Bring everything to a boil, then reduce the heat to a low simmer. Cook for 30 minutes or until the liquid has almost evaporated.

Heat a heavy-based frying pan over high heat and add the oil. As it begins to smoke, add the beefsteaks and sear them until the uncooked surface looks slightly bloody. Turn the steaks over and cook for an additional 1 minute before taking the pan off the heat. Season the steaks and let them sit for a few minutes in the pan.

Add the oyster mushrooms and butter to the onion mixture. Cook 1 minute more. Serve the steaks on warmed plates with a salad of cannellini beans and chopped basil, and spoon the onion sauce over the steaks.

bell pepper and potato stew with saffron

serves 4

3 tablespoons butter

2 red onions, diced

2 garlic cloves, crushed

1 large pinch saffron threads

1 3/4 cups canned chopped tomatoes

1 teaspoon sugar

4 boiling potatoes, cut into
  bite-size pieces

1 red bell pepper, cut into thick strips

1 teaspoon thyme leaves

sea salt and freshly ground black
  pepper, to season

1 large handful cilantro leaves

1/2 cup finely chopped chives

Heat the butter, onions, garlic, and saffron together in a large saucepan over medium heat. When the onions are soft and transparent, add the tomatoes, sugar, and 2 cups of water. Cover with a lid and simmer for 10 minutes. Add the potatoes, bell pepper, and thyme. Then cover and simmer for an additional 35 minutes. Season with sea salt and freshly ground black pepper and serve sprinkled with the cilantro and chives.

roasted lamb

3¹/₄-pound leg of lamb
olive oil
salt and freshly ground black pepper,
   for rub
5 garlic cloves, halved
10 sprigs rosemary

Preheat the oven to 400°F. With the point of a small sharp knife, make several incisions into the skin of the leg of lamb. Rub the surface of the meat with a little olive oil and then rub salt and freshly ground black pepper into the skin. Press the garlic into the incisions. Sprinkle the rosemary over the base of a roasting pan and put the lamb on top. Bake for 30 minutes, then spoon some of the juices from the pan over the lamb. Bake for an additional 40 minutes. Transfer the lamb to a warm platter, cover with foil, and allow it to rest for 15 minutes before carving. Serve with roasted vegetables and fresh mint sauce.

red mullet with tomato and fennel sauce

serves 4

2 teaspoons sea salt

2 teaspoons fennel seeds

20 mint leaves

1 tablespoon olive oil

4 ripe tomatoes, finely chopped

1/2 cup white wine

2 small fennel bulbs, thinly sliced

four 6-ounce whole red mullet, gutted and scaled

2 tablespoons extra-virgin olive oil

freshly ground black pepper, to season

Preheat the oven to 350°F. Put the sea salt, fennel seeds, and mint leaves in a mortar and pestle or small blender and grind them together. When the leaves and seeds have begun to break down, add the olive oil to make a thin paste.

Put half of the tomatoes, all the wine, and half the fennel into a casserole dish. (Use two dishes, if necessary, to fit the fish.) Rinse the mullet in cold water and dry with paper towels. Rub with the fennel paste, then put the fish on top of the tomatoes. Stuff some of the remaining fennel into the fish cavities and sprinkle the rest over the fish, along with the remaining tomatoes. Cover with a lid and bake for 25 minutes.

To serve, carefully remove the whole fish and put them on warmed serving plates. Spoon the sauce over the fish, drizzle with olive oil, and season with freshly ground black pepper.

linguine with shrimp and fresh herbs

14 ounces linguine

1/3 cup light olive oil

3 garlic cloves, crushed and finely chopped

16 raw jumbo shrimp, peeled and deveined, with tails intact

2 cups cherry tomatoes, halved

1 handful Italian parsley, roughly chopped

12 basil leaves, torn

1/2 cup chives

juice of 1 lemon

sea salt and freshly ground black pepper, to season

Bring a saucepan of salted water to a boil. Add the linguine and cook in rapidly boiling water until al dente.

Meanwhile, put the olive oil in a frying pan and heat over medium heat. Add the garlic, stir briefly, then add the shrimp. Fry the shrimp until they are pink on both sides and have begun to curl up. Add the cherry tomatoes and cook for an additional 1 minute. Remove from the heat.

Strain the cooked linguine and return it to the saucepan. Add the shrimp and tomato mixture, herbs, and lemon juice. Toss together. Season with sea salt and freshly ground black pepper.

pastry twists panettone fingers with rhubarb spiced biscotti with marsala mascarpone chocolate pots with chocolate wafers ice cream shots with sweet liqueur fresh fig tarts chocolate truffles florentines tiny tiramisu chocolate creams fig surprise chocolate samosas chocolate caramel "brûlées" strawberries with nutty phyllo chocolate brownies figs in sauternes with crème fraîche parfait chocolate

04 sweets

pudding chocolate nut meringues with cream and berries rich chocolate cake chocolate marquise strawberry rice pudding chocolate cupcakes chocolate and hazelnut bars summer berries with crème anglaise butterfly cake hazelnut meringue with

pastry twists

2 teaspoons ground cinnamon
1/4 cup superfine sugar
1/2 sheet ready-prepared puff pastry
1 tablespoon unsalted butter, melted

Place the cinnamon and sugar in a small bowl and stir to combine. Cut the pastry into twelve 1/4-inch thick strips, then cut the lengths in half again. Place each of the strips onto a cookie sheet lined with parchment paper, brush with melted butter, and sprinkle with some of the cinnamon sugar. Preheat the oven to 315°F.

Gently twist each strip of pastry to form loose spirals. Sprinkle with any remaining sugar. Refrigerate the pastry twists for 10 minutes. Bake for 10–12 minutes or until lightly golden. Cool on a wire rack. Serve with hot chocolate, if desired.

panettone fingers with rhubarb

makes 12

6 stems rhubarb, trimmed

1/2 teaspoon grated fresh ginger

1 teaspoon finely chopped orange zest

4 tablespoons orange juice

1/2 vanilla bean, split and scraped

1/4 cup soft brown sugar

1 tablespoon unsalted butter

12 fingers panettone, cut into
   5 x 3/4-inch lengths

confectioners' sugar, for dusting

Preheat the oven to 350°F. Cut each rhubarb stem into two 5-inch lengths.

Place the ginger, orange zest, orange juice, vanilla bean, brown sugar, and butter in a roasting pan and place in the oven for 1–2 minutes or until the butter has fully melted. Remove from the oven and stir to combine. Add the rhubarb and toss so that the rhubarb is thoroughly coated in the sugary mixture. Return the pan to the oven and bake for 10 minutes. Gently turn the rhubarb over and cook for an additional 10 minutes. Allow to cool.

Toast each of the panettone fingers under a broiler until golden and place a strip of rhubarb along each one. Drizzle with the syrup, sprinkle with confectioners' sugar, and serve.

spiced biscotti with marsala mascarpone

makes approximately 120 cookies

2 cups all-purpose flour
1 cup superfine sugar
2 teaspoons baking powder
heaping 1/2 cup sliced dried figs
heaping 1/4 cup dried apricots, sliced
1 2/3 cups slivered almonds
2 teaspoons chopped lemon zest
1/4 teaspoon ground cardamom
1 teaspoon ground cinnamon
3 eggs, beaten

Marsala mascarpone
heaping 3/4 cup mascarpone
2 tablespoons sweet Marsala
1 tablespoon superfine sugar

Preheat the oven to 350°F. Mix the flour, sugar, baking powder, dried fruit, almonds, lemon zest, cardamom, and cinnamon in a bowl. Make a well in the center. Fold in the eggs to make a sticky dough. Divide into four pieces. Roll out each portion of the dough to form logs 1 1/2 inches in diameter. Place the logs on a cookie sheet lined with parchment paper, leaving space between each log to spread. Bake for 30 minutes. Remove and allow to cool. Reduce the oven temperature to 275°F.

With a bread knife, cut each of the loaves into thin 1/4-inch wide slices. Lay the biscotti on a cookie sheet and return to the oven. Bake for 20 minutes, turning the biscotti once. Remove from the oven and cool on wire racks.

Put the mascarpone, Marsala, and superfine sugar in a bowl and mix until smooth. Serve the biscotti with the mascarpone mixture.

chocolate pots with chocolate wafers

chocolate pots

1 1/4 cups light whipping cream

1 1/3 cups roughly chopped dark
chocolate

pinch salt

1/2 teaspoon natural vanilla extract

1/2 teaspoon ground cardamom

1 egg

chocolate wafers

heaping 1/4 cup superfine sugar

3 1/2 cups unsalted butter, softened

2 egg whites

1/3 cup all-purpose flour

4 teaspoons dark unsweetened cocoa
powder, plus extra for dusting

To make the chocolate pots, heat the cream and chocolate in a double boiler over low heat. Allow the chocolate to melt, stirring occasionally. Add salt with the vanilla and cardamom. Whisk in the egg. Continue to whisk over low heat until smooth. Pour the mixture into six 1/2-cup pots and chill for 3 hours.

To make the wafers, whisk the sugar and butter until light and creamy. Slowly add the egg whites, then the flour and cocoa. Chill for 1 hour. Preheat the oven to 350°F.

Line a cookie sheet with parchment paper and, using the back of a spoon, spread 1 tablespoon of the mixture into a thin 4-inch circle. Repeat, leaving a little space between wafers. Bake for 15 minutes. Remove from the oven and carefully lift the wafers from the sheet with a spatula. Allow to cool on a wire rack. Dust with cocoa powder and serve with the chocolate pots.

ice cream shots with sweet liqueur

serves 6

12 small scoops hazelnut ice cream
1/2 cup grated dark chocolate
1/3 cup Frangelico

Divide the ice cream and chocolate among six small glasses and top with the liqueur.

Note—You can use any number of ice cream and liqueur combinations: for example, chocolate ice cream with Tia Maria, coffee ice cream with crème de cacao, or vanilla ice cream with Grand Marnier.

fresh fig tarts

1/4 cup honey

heaping 1/2 cup mascarpone

12 prebaked short-crust tart shells
   (see basics)

3 fresh figs, thinly sliced

1/3 cup roughly chopped toasted
   hazelnuts

confectioners' sugar, for dusting

Place the honey and mascarpone in a
bowl and blend with a spoon until the
mixture is smooth. Spoon into the
pastry shells. Top with the thinly sliced
fresh fig and a scattering of hazelnuts.
Sprinkle with confectioners' sugar
and serve.

chocolate truffles

heaping 3/4 cup chopped dark
  chocolate
1/4 cup sour cream
2 teaspoons finely grated orange zest
1/8 teaspoon ground cardamom
1/4 cup unsweetened cocoa powder

Place the chocolate in a bowl over a saucepan of simmering water. When the chocolate has melted, fold in the sour cream, orange zest, and cardamom. Stir well, then place in the refrigerator for 30 minutes or until set.

Place the cocoa powder in a shallow bowl. Drop a teaspoon at a time of the chocolate mixture into the cocoa. Toss to cover the chocolate with the cocoa, then roll the chocolate into a ball in the palm of your hand, covering the outside with more cocoa. When all the truffles have been rolled, place in an airtight container in the refrigerator until ready to serve.

florentines

2 tablespoons raisins, finely chopped

2 tablespoons finely chopped
   preserved ginger

1 cup flaked almonds

heaping 1/3 cup unsalted butter

1/2 cup superfine sugar

2/3 cup chopped dark chocolate

Preheat the oven to 350°F. Line two cookie sheets with parchment paper. Put the raisins in a bowl with the ginger and almonds. Melt the butter and sugar in a saucepan over low heat. When the sugar has dissolved, turn up the heat and allow the mixture to bubble for 1 minute. Pour the hot mixture into the bowl and quickly stir to combine all the ingredients.

Drop teaspoons of the mixture onto the cookie sheets, allowing room for the florentines to spread considerably. Bake for 10 minutes. Allow the florentines to cool on the sheets for 5 minutes before carefully lifting them onto a wire rack to cool completely.

Place the chocolate in a bowl over a pan of simmering water. When it has melted, use a pastry brush to paint the chocolate onto the underside of the florentines.

tiny tiramisu

coffee syrup

2 tablespoons sugar
1/2 cup strong black coffee
1/2 cup Tia Maria

coffee cupcakes

1/4 cup strong black coffee
2 eggs
heaping 1/3 cup unsalted butter,
   softened
3/4 cup sugar
1 1/2 cups all-purpose flour
2 teaspoons baking powder
1/4 cup ground almonds
1/4 cup unsweetened cocoa powder,
   for dusting

mascarpone filling

1 tablespoon sugar
2 egg yolks
1/2 cup Marsala
heaping 1 cup mascarpone

Make a coffee syrup by bringing the sugar and coffee to a boil in a small saucepan. Simmer for 5 minutes. Remove, allow to cool, then stir in the Tia Maria.

To make the cupcakes, preheat the oven to 350°F. Place all the cupcake ingredients in a food processor and blend until smooth. Put tablespoons of the mixture into two 12-hole mini muffin pans and bake for 12 minutes. Cool on wire racks.

Make the filling by placing the sugar, egg yolks, and Marsala in a bowl over a saucepan of simmering water and whisking until frothy. Remove and chill. Fold through the mascarpone. With a small knife, remove the lids from the cakes, cutting a well in the center. Spoon a tablespoon of coffee syrup, then a tablespoon of the mascarpone, into the top of each cake. Replace the tops of the cakes and dust with cocoa powder. Allow to sit for several hours before serving.

chocolate creams   makes 40 cookies

1 1/4 cups all-purpose flour
2 tablespoons Dutch cocoa powder,
   plus extra, for dusting
1/4 teaspoon salt
1 teaspoon baking powder
heaping 1/3 cup unsalted butter
1 1/4 cups chopped dark chocolate
1/2 cup superfine sugar
2 eggs

chocolate cream
2/3 cup chopped chocolate
2 tablespoons light whipping cream

Sift together the flour, cocoa, baking powder, and salt into a bowl. Melt the butter and chocolate in a bowl over a saucepan of simmering water, stirring until smooth. Remove from the heat. Add the sugar, stirring until dissolved. Stir in the eggs, one at a time, until well combined, then fold through the dry ingredients. Refrigerate the mixture for 20 minutes or until just firm.

Make the chocolate cream by heating the chocolate and cream in a bowl over a saucepan of simmering water, stirring until smooth. Remove from the heat and allow to cool.

Preheat the oven to 350°F. Pipe teaspoon-size buttons of the cookie batter onto cookie sheets lined with parchment paper. Bake for 5–7 minutes or until firm. Cool slightly on the sheet before transferring to a wire rack.

Stick the bases of the cookies together with the chocolate cream and lightly dust with cocoa. Store in an airtight container.

fig surprise

3 fresh figs
2 teaspoons finely chopped
  candied ginger
2 tablespoons soft brown sugar
1/4 teaspoon grated lemon zest
1/4 teaspoon ground cinnamon
3 sheets phyllo pastry
1/4 cup unsalted butter, melted
confectioners' sugar, for dusting
vanilla or honey ice cream, to serve

Preheat the oven to 400°F. Cut each fig into eight wedges. In a small bowl, combine the candied ginger, brown sugar, lemon zest, and cinnamon. Stir to combine. Cut each sheet of phyllo into eight equal pieces. Take one sheet and lightly brush it with the melted butter. Place a piece of fig against the side so that the stem end is outside the pastry. Place a little of the brown sugar mixture onto the fig. Fold the phyllo around the fig, leaving the stem section free. Repeat with the other pieces of pastry and fig.

Place the wrapped figs onto a cookie sheet lined with parchment paper. Bake for 7–10 minutes or until golden brown. Cool on a wire rack. Sprinkle with confectioners' sugar and serve warm with vanilla or honey ice cream.

chocolate samosas

makes 24

1 egg yolk

12 wonton wrappers

heaping 3/4 cup finely chopped milk
   chocolate

1/2 cup toasted hazelnuts, roughly
   chopped

2 bananas, sliced

2 cups vegetable oil

confectioners' sugar, to serve

heavy cream, to serve

Whisk the egg yolk with 2 tablespoons of water in a bowl. Lay the wonton wrappers on a dry, clean surface and put some chocolate, hazelnuts, and banana slices in the center of each one. Brush the edges of the wonton wrappers with a little of the egg wash and twist the edges together. Put the wontons on a plate, cover with plastic wrap, and refrigerate until needed.

Heat the oil in a deep-based frying pan or saucepan until it begins to shimmer. Put the wontons into the hot oil, a few at a time, and cook until golden. Remove and drain on paper towels. Repeat with the remaining wontons. Sprinkle with confectioners' sugar and serve hot with a generous dollop of thick cream.

chocolate caramel "brûlées"

serves 10

1½ cups light whipping cream
1 cup milk
1 vanilla bean, split and scraped
5 egg yolks
¾ cup sugar
pinch salt
¼ cup grated dark chocolate
Dutch cocoa powder, for dusting

Preheat the oven to 300°F. Place the cream, milk, and vanilla bean in a saucepan and heat until almost boiling. Remove from the heat.

In a bowl, beat the egg yolks with ¼ cup of the sugar and the pinch of salt until thick. Place the remaining sugar in a heavy-based saucepan. Melt it over medium heat. When it has become a golden color, pour over the hot milk. Whisk until the toffeed sugar has dissolved, then pour over the egg mixture. Whisk to combine. Strain and pour into ten ½-cup ramekins. Place in a roasting pan and fill the pan with hot water until the water comes two-thirds of the way up the side of the ramekins. Cover with foil and bake for 20–25 minutes. Remove from the oven and uncover.

Sprinkle the grated chocolate over the top of the custards until the surface is covered. Wipe the edges of the ramekins clean. Allow to cool. Serve sprinkled with cocoa powder.

strawberries with nutty phyllo

serves 4

1/3 cup flaked almonds
1/4 cup pistachio nuts
2 tablespoons honey
1 teaspoon grated lemon zest
1 tablespoon lemon juice
4 sheets phyllo pastry
3 tablespoons unsalted butter, melted
1 teaspoon cinnamon
confectioners' sugar
2 cups strawberries, hulled and halved
cardamom and rosewater syrup
  (see basics)

Preheat the oven to 350°F. Finely chop the almonds and pistachios and put them in a small bowl along with the honey and lemon zest and juice. Put a piece of parchment paper on a greased cookie sheet. Lay one of the phyllo sheets on top, brush the sheet with a little melted butter, and then lay another sheet on top. Brush the top sheet with butter and sprinkle with the cinnamon and the nut mixture. Top with the two final buttered sheets of pastry.

Bake the phyllo for 15 minutes or until it is golden brown, then cover the top with sifted confectioners' sugar and break it into rough pieces.

Divide the strawberries among four plates. Top with the pastry. Drizzle with the cardamom and rosewater syrup.

chocolate brownies

makes 35 squares

1/2 cup unsalted butter

heaping 3/4 cup chopped dark
chocolate

4 eggs

1 1/3 cups superfine sugar

1 cup all-purpose flour

1/4 cup Dutch cocoa powder

1 teaspoon natural vanilla extract

heaping 1/2 cup roughly ground
hazelnuts

pinch salt

confectioners' sugar or unsweetened
cocoa powder, to serve

Preheat the oven to 350°F. Melt the butter and chocolate in a medium-sized saucepan over low heat, stirring occasionally, until smooth. Allow to cool for 10 minutes. Beat the eggs and sugar in a large bowl until light and fluffy, then gradually add the cooled chocolate mixture. Fold in the flour, cocoa powder, vanilla extract, hazelnuts, and salt. Pour into a greased 12 x 8-inch baking pan lined with parchment paper. Bake for 30 minutes or until the cake edges begin to pull away from the pan. Allow to cool in the pan. Cut into squares and dust with confectioners' sugar or unsweetened cocoa to serve.

figs in sauternes with crème fraîche parfait serves 6

12 fresh figs, quartered
1 1/2 cups Sauternes
1 teaspoon honey

parfait
5 egg yolks
heaping 1/2 cup superfine sugar
1 teaspoon natural vanilla extract
2 cups crème fraîche

Put the figs in a bowl and cover with the Sauternes. Drizzle with honey. Cover and refrigerate for 12 hours or overnight.

Whisk the egg yolks, sugar, and vanilla extract until the mixture is thick and very pale. Fold the crème fraîche through, then spoon into a 8 1/2 x 3 1/4- inch pan lined with parchment paper. Freeze until firm. Slice the parfait into six thick slices and serve on chilled plates with the quartered figs and a spoonful of the Sauternes.

chocolate pudding

1/2 cup unsweetened cocoa powder,
    plus extra for dusting
1/2 cup soft brown sugar
2 eggs
2/3 cup superfine sugar
31/2 tablespoons unsalted butter,
    chopped
2/3 cup chopped dark chocolate
1/2 cup milk
1 cup sifted self-raising flour
cream or custard, to serve

Preheat the oven to 350°F. Butter six 11/4-cups ramekins. Put 1/3 cup of the cocoa powder, the brown sugar, and 11/4 cups of boiling water in a large pitcher.

Put the eggs and superfine sugar in a large bowl and lightly beat together.

Heat the butter, chocolate, and milk in a small saucepan over medium heat for 3 minutes or until the butter and chocolate have melted. Remove from the heat and cool slightly.

Add the flour and remaining cocoa powder to the beaten egg mixture and then stir in the melted chocolate. Divide the batter among the ramekins and spoon the hot water mixture over the puddings. Transfer to a cookie sheet and bake for 30 minutes or until firm. Dust with cocoa and serve with cream or warm custard.

chocolate nut meringues with cream and berries serves 6

3 egg whites
heaping 3/4 cups superfine sugar
2 tablespoons dark cocoa powder
2 tablespoons ground hazelnuts
1/2 cup flaked almonds
scant 2/3 cup light whipping cream
3 cups mixed berries

Preheat the oven to 300°F. Line a large cookie sheet with parchment paper. Whisk the egg whites until they form soft peaks and then slowly add the sugar, continuing to beat until the mixture is white and glossy. Fold in the cocoa and ground hazelnuts, then spoon the meringue into six large dollops onto the cookie sheet. Using the back of the spoon, create a dip in the top of each meringue. Sprinkle with the almonds and bake for 45 minutes. Turn off the heat, but leave the meringues to cool in the oven with the door ajar. Store in an airtight container until ready to use. Serve topped with whipped cream and berries.

rich chocolate cake   serves 10

1 cup unsalted butter
1 1/3 cups chopped dark chocolate
1 1/2 cups strong coffee
2 cups superfine sugar
1 1/2 cups all-purpose flour
1 teaspoon baking powder
1/4 cup unsweetened cocoa powder
2 eggs
2 teaspoons natural vanilla extract
1 quantity chocolate frosting (see
   basics)
whipped cream or vanilla ice cream,
   to serve

Preheat the oven to 350°F. Grease and line a 10-inch springform pan. Put the butter, chocolate, and coffee in a saucepan over low heat. Cook until the chocolate melts. Add the sugar and stir to dissolve. Remove from the heat and pour into a bowl. Whisk in the dry ingredients, then add the eggs and vanilla extract. Whisk to combine.

Pour the batter into the prepared pan and bake for 1 hour. Allow the cake to cool in the pan before removing. Cover with chocolate frosting. Serve with whipped cream or vanilla ice cream.

chocolate marquise   serves 4-6

2/3 cup chopped dark chocolate
31/2 tablespoons unsalted butter,
   softened
1/4 cup superfine sugar
2 tablespoons unsweetened cocoa
   powder
2 egg yolks
1 teaspoon rosewater
scant 2/3 cup light whipping cream
11/4 cups raspberries, to serve
6 white nectarines, sliced, to serve
1/2 cup flaked almonds, toasted,
   to serve
confectioners' sugar, for dusting

Melt the chocolate in a heatproof bowl set over a saucepan of boiling water, making sure the base does not touch the water. Beat the butter with half the sugar until pale and fluffy. Mix in the cocoa. Beat the egg yolks with the remaining sugar until pale and smooth, then add the rosewater. Whip the cream until thick.

Mix the melted chocolate into the butter mixture, fold in the egg mixture, and then fold in the cream. Spoon into a lined 81/2 x 31/4-inch pan and chill for 3 hours or until set.

Turn out the marquise and cut into thick slices. Serve with the raspberries, nectarines, toasted flaked almonds, and a dusting of confectioners' sugar.

strawberry rice pudding

makes 10 small or 6 regular servings

2 cups milk

$1/4$ cup sugar

2 teaspoons finely chopped orange
   zest

3 cardamom pods

pinch salt

$1/3$ cup short-grained rice

$1/2$ cup cream, whipped

scant $1/2$ cup chopped pistachios

2 cups strawberries

confectioners' sugar, for dusting

Bring the milk to a boil with the sugar, orange zest, cardamom pods, and salt, then tip in the rice. Reduce the heat and simmer gently for 30 minutes or until the rice is cooked. Remove the cardamom pods. Allow the rice to cool, then fold in the cream and half of the pistachios. Layer the rice and strawberries in small bowls, starting with the rice, then fruit, and so on. Top with a sprinkle of the remaining pistachios and dust with confectioners' sugar.

chocolate cupcakes

1/2 cup unsalted butter
2/3 cup chopped dark chocolate
3/4 cup strong coffee
1 cup sugar
1 egg
1 teaspoon natural vanilla extract
3/4 cup all-purpose flour
1 teaspoon baking powder
1/4 cup unsweetened cocoa powder
1 quantity chocolate frosting (see basics)
whipped cream or vanilla ice cream, to serve

Preheat the oven to 350°F. Put the butter, chocolate, and coffee in a saucepan over low heat and leave it until the chocolate has melted. Add the sugar, stirring until it has dissolved, then pour the chocolate mixture into a bowl. Whisk in the egg and vanilla extract before sifting in the flour, baking powder, and cocoa powder. Stir together.

Spoon the mixture into a 12-hole muffin pan lined with paper muffin cups and bake for 15 minutes. Allow the cakes to cool before removing them. Frost the cakes and serve with whipped cream or vanilla ice cream.

chocolate and hazelnut bars

makes 20 pieces

1 cup unsalted butter
1 1/2 cups sugar
3/4 cup unsweetened cocoa powder,
　plus extra for dusting
1/3 cup all-purpose flour
1/2 teaspoon baking powder
pinch salt
4 eggs
1 cup chopped toasted hazelnuts
1 1/3 cups chopped chocolate or
　chocolate chips

Preheat the oven to 350°F. Grease and line a 9-inch square cake pan. Melt the butter with the sugar in a saucepan over low heat. When the butter has melted, stir to ensure that the sugar has completely dissolved. Remove the saucepan from the heat. Sift the cocoa powder, flour, and baking powder into a large bowl and add the pinch of salt. Make a well in the center and stir in the melted butter and sugar, then stir in the eggs. Add the hazelnuts and chocolate. Stir to combine, then pour into the prepared cake pan. Bake for 25–30 minutes. Remove from the oven and cool in the pan. Cut into pieces and dust with cocoa.

summer berries with crème anglaise

1 cup milk
1 cup light whipping cream
1 vanilla bean
5 egg yolks
1/3 cup superfine sugar
4 cups mixed raspberries, blackberries, and blueberries

Put the milk and cream into a heavy-based saucepan. Lightly rub the vanilla bean between your fingers to soften it. With the point of a small sharp knife, cut the bean in half lengthwise and add it to the saucepan. Heat the saucepan over medium heat and bring the milk and cream just to simmering point. Remove from the heat.

Whisk the egg yolks with the sugar in a bowl until light and foamy. Whisk a little of the warm milk and cream into the eggs. Add the remaining liquid, reserving the vanilla bean. Whisk to combine. Rinse the saucepan and return the mixture to the saucepan.

Cook over medium heat, stirring constantly with a wooden spoon, until the mixture thickens and coats the back of the spoon. Strain into a bowl. Scrape the vanilla seeds from the split bean into the custard. Stir the specks of vanilla through the custard. Pour into a serving pitcher and serve with the mixed berries.

butterfly cakes

heaping 2/3 cup unsalted butter,
  softened
3/4 cup superfine sugar
3 eggs
1/2 cup milk
1 teaspoon natural vanilla extract
11/2 cups self-raising flour, sifted
1 cup light whipping cream
6 strawberries, quartered
confectioners' sugar, for dusting

Preheat the oven to 350°F. Line a 12-hole muffin pan with paper muffin cups. Beat the butter with the sugar in a mixing bowl until pale and creamy. Add the eggs, milk, and vanilla. Stir to combine, then fold in the flour. Spoon the batter into the muffin cups and bake for 15–20 minutes or until firm and golden. Transfer the cupcakes to a wire rack to cool.

Cut shallow rounds from the center of each cake using the point of a sharp knife, then cut the rounds in half. Whip the cream, spoon into each cavity, and position the two halves of each cake in the cream to resemble butterfly wings. Top with the quartered strawberries and dust with confectioners' sugar.

hazelnut meringue with berries

serves 6

2 egg whites
1/2 cup superfine sugar
1/3 cup ground hazelnuts
1 1/4 cups light whipping cream
1 teaspoon natural vanilla extract
3 2/3 cups mixed raspberries, blackberries, blueberries, and strawberries, cut into small pieces

Preheat the oven to 300°F. Whisk the egg whites until they form soft peaks and then slowly add the sugar, continuing to beat until the mixture is stiff. Fold in the hazelnuts.

Line two cookie sheets with waxed paper and divide the meringue mixture between them, placing a big dollop in the middle of each sheet. Using the back of a spoon, spread the mixture out until you have two 8-inch circles of meringue.

Bake for 40 minutes. Turn the oven off, but leave the meringues in the oven with the door ajar for 30 minutes.

Whip the cream and fold in the vanilla extract. When the meringues are cool, put one of the rounds on a serving plate. Top with some of the cream and half the berries, arranging them so that they make a flat surface for the next meringue layer. Put the other meringue on top and decorate with the cream and remaining berries. Allow to sit for 15 minutes before serving.

mini danish

1 sheet ready-prepared puff pastry
1 egg
3 tablespoons milk
4 small plums, cut into eight wedges
confectioners' sugar, for dusting

pastry cream
1/4 cup superfine sugar
2 egg yolks
1/4 cup cornstarch
1 vanilla bean
1 cup milk
1 1/2 tablespoons unsalted butter

To make the pastry cream, whisk the sugar, egg yolks, and cornstarch in a bowl. Split open the vanilla bean.Place it in a saucepan with the milk. Slowly bring to a boil, then remove from the heat. Whisk 1/3 cup of the hot milk into the egg mixture. Tip this mixture back into the saucepan containing the remainder of the milk, and whisk. Return the pan to the heat. Bring back to a boil, stirring. Boil for 1 minute, then pass through a sieve into a bowl. Discard the vanilla bean. Add the butter and stir until melted. Allow the pastry cream to cool, then cover with plastic wrap and refrigerate.

Preheat the oven to 350°F. Cut the sheet of pastry into 16 small squares. Beat the egg and milk together and set aside. Place each of the squares into a shallow muffin pan. Prick the pastry bases with a fork and fill with a teaspoon of pastry cream. Top with sliced plums. Fold the pastry over the fruit to enclose it, then glaze with the egg wash. Bake for 12 minutes or until golden. Serve warm or at room temperature. Dust with confectioners' sugar.

coconut, raspberry, and white chocolate bars
makes 20 bars

1/2 cup unsalted butter
1 cup chopped white chocolate
3/4 cup superfine sugar
1 cup self-rising flour
1 cup dried coconut
2 eggs, beaten
1 1/4 cups fresh raspberries
confectioners' sugar, for dusting

Preheat the oven to 350°F. Grease and line a 10 1/2 x 6 1/4-inch pan. Melt the butter and white chocolate in a saucepan over low heat. Add the sugar and stir to combine. Pour into a large bowl and add the flour and dried coconut. Stir to combine, then add the eggs. Stir lightly to just combine, then fold in the raspberries. Pour the mixture into the prepared pan and bake for 40 minutes or until firm. Allow to cool in the pan. Cut into 20 pieces and dust with confectioners' sugar.

chocolate chip cookies makes 20

1/2 cup unsalted butter, softened
1 cup soft brown sugar
1 teaspoon natural vanilla extract
1 tablespoon milk
1 egg, beaten
1 1/2 cups all-purpose flour, sifted
1 teaspoon baking powder, sifted
1 1/2 cups dark chocolate chips

Preheat the oven to 350°F. Grease and line a cookie sheet with waxed paper. Beat the butter with the brown sugar in a bowl until light and creamy. Add the vanilla extract, milk, and egg and work them lightly into the butter mixture. Gently fold in the flour and baking powder. Stir in the chocolate chips. Drop heaping tablespoons of the mixture onto the cookie sheet, leaving about 1 1/4 inches between each cookie. Bake for 15 minutes or until lightly golden. Transfer the cookies to a wire rack to cool. Store in an airtight container.

raspberry ripple cake serves 10

2 cups frozen raspberries
2 cups all-purpose flour
2 teaspoons baking powder
1/4 teaspoon salt
1/2 cup unsalted butter, softened
1 cup superfine sugar
3 eggs, lightly beaten
1 cup sour cream
1 1/2 tablespoons butter, melted
1 cup confectioners' sugar, sifted

Preheat the oven to 350°F. Grease and line a 9-inch springform pan. Put the frozen raspberries into a bowl and lightly crush them. Reserve about 1 tablespoon of their juice in another bowl to make the frosting.

Sift the flour, baking powder, and salt into a large bowl. Cream the butter and sugar until pale and fluffy, then stir in the eggs. Add the dry ingredients, alternating with the sour cream, and mixing well after each addition. Spoon one-third of the batter into the prepared pan, then spoon over half the raspberries. Repeat with another third of the batter and the remaining raspberries. Top with the remaining batter. Bake for 50 minutes or until a skewer put into the center of the cake comes out clean. Allow the cake to cool in the pan before turning out and frosting it.

To make the frosting, add the melted butter to the reserved raspberry juice. Slowly stir in the confectioners' sugar until the frosting has a smooth runny consistency. Spoon over the cake.

fig and burned butter tart

6 fresh figs
1 prebaked short-crust tart shell (see basics)
3 eggs
3/4 cup superfine sugar
1/4 cup all-purpose flour
3/4 cup unsalted butter

Preheat the oven to 350°F. Slice the figs into quarters and arrange them in the tart shell with the narrow ends pointing up.

Beat the eggs and sugar until they are pale and fluffy, then fold in the flour. Heat the butter in a saucepan over high heat, and when it begins to froth and turn light brown, pour the hot butter into the egg mixture and continue to beat for 1 minute. Pour the filling over the figs and bake for 25 minutes or until the filling is cooked and golden brown. Allow to cool before serving.

chocolate ice cream   serves 4

1¹/₂ cups milk
1 cup light whipping cream
²/₃ cup roughly chopped dark
  chocolate
4 egg yolks
¹/₃ cup superfine sugar
2 tablespoons unsweetened cocoa
  powder

Put the milk, cream, and chocolate in a heavy-based saucepan over medium heat. Bring the milk and cream just to simmering point, stirring to help melt the chocolate. Remove the saucepan from the heat.

Put the egg yolks and sugar in a mixing bowl and whisk until light and foamy. Add the cocoa powder and whisk again. Whisk in a little of the warm chocolate mixture, then add the remaining liquid and whisk to combine. Return the mixture to the cleaned saucepan. Cook over medium heat, stirring constantly with a wooden spoon, until the mixture thickens and coats the back of the spoon. Strain into a bowl and allow to cool. Churn in an ice-cream machine according to the manufacturer's instructions.

bloody mary whiskey sour rose petal sherbert sangria watermelon and chili cooler bellini strawberry lassi cosmopolitan brandy alexander campari classic champagne cocktail sour cherry blossom watermelon, mint, and vodka rhubarb, strawberry, and white rum chiller mexican shot ripe cherry whiskey sour rose petal sherbet sorbet vodka shot bloody mary brandy alexander strawberry lassi cosmopolitan ripe cherry

05   drinks

rhubarb, strawberry, and white rum chiller watermelon and chili cooler bellini champagne cocktail sour cherry blossom sangria watermelon, mint, and vodka mexican shot bloody mary campari classic rose petal sherbet brandy alexander strawberry lassi champagne

bloody mary

2 small tomatoes, finely chopped
1/4 teaspoon salt
1/3 cup tomato juice
2 fluid ounces vodka
1/4 teaspoon Worcestershire sauce
1/4 teaspoon Tabasco sauce
1 teaspoon horseradish cream
1 teaspoon lime juice
ice cubes, to serve
celery, lime, and freshly ground black
   pepper, to garnish

Put the tomatoes and salt in a bowl and allow to sit for 30 minutes. Put the tomato pieces in a blender with the tomato juice and blend until smooth. Pour the tomato juice into a shaker and add the vodka, Worcestershire sauce, Tabasco sauce, horseradish cream, and lime juice and shake vigorously. Pour over ice and garnish with a celery stalk, a slice of lime, and freshly ground black pepper.

strawberry lassi

serves 2

1 cup hulled strawberries
1 cup yogurt
1 teaspoon honey
8 ice cubes

Combine the strawberries, yogurt, honey, and ice cubes in a blender. Blend until smooth and pour into chilled glasses.

ripe cherry

2 fluid ounces framboise
1 fluid ounce Malibu
1 fluid ounce white crème de cacao
crushed ice, to serve

Put all the ingredients except the ice in a cocktail shaker and shake well. Pour over the crushed ice and serve immediately.

watermelon and chili cooler

serves 2

chili syrup
2 large red chilies
1/2 cup sugar

2 cups watermelon juice
2 tablespoons lime juice
mint sprigs, to garnish
ice cubes, to serve

To make the chili syrup, put the chilies, sugar, and 1/2 cup of water in a small saucepan and bring to a boil. Reduce the heat and simmer for 5 minutes. Remove the chilies. Cool the syrup and place in a clean jar or bottle. Store in the refrigerator until ready to use.

Blend together the watermelon juice, 2 tablespoons of the chili syrup, and the lime juice. Pour into glasses filled with ice cubes and garnish with sprigs of fresh mint.

rose petal sherbet   serves 8

4 red organic roses, petals removed
1 cup sugar
1 tablespoon rosewater
8 cups sparkling mineral water

Put the petals, sugar, and 1¼ cups water in a large saucepan and bring to a boil. Reduce the heat and simmer for 8 minutes or until a light syrup has been made. Remove any film as it forms. Cool and stir in the rosewater. To serve, pour the syrup into chilled glasses and top with sparkling mineral water.

sangria

1 bottle of Rioja or other light red wine
7 tablespoons sugar syrup
2 fluid ounces Cointreau
1/4 cup lemon juice
1 orange, thinly sliced
1 lime, thinly sliced
ice cubes, to serve

In a large pitcher, put the Rioja, sugar syrup, Cointreau, lemon juice, orange, and lime. Stir all the ingredients well and top with ice.

sorbet vodka shot   serves 6

6 tablespoons fruit sorbet
4 fluid ounces vodka

Divide the fruit sorbet between six chilled shot glasses and pour a tablespoon of vodka over each.

mexican shot

3 fluid ounces tequila
6 tablespoons tomato juice
2 plum tomatoes, roughly chopped,
  plus 1, finely diced
1 teaspoon lime juice
2 tablespoons finely chopped
  cilantro leaves

chili syrup
2 large red chilies
1/2 cup sugar

To make the chili syrup, put the chilies, sugar, and 1/2 cup of water in a saucepan. Bring to a boil. Reduce the heat and simmer for 5 minutes. Remove the chilies. Cool the syrup and place in a jar or bottle. Store in the refrigerator until ready to use.

Put the tequila, tomato juice, chopped tomatoes, 1 tablespoon of the chili syrup, and the lime juice in a blender and mix until smooth. Pour into a small container and fold in the diced tomato and cilantro. Place in the freezer for several hours or overnight. Break up with a fork, or place in a blender and pulse. Spoon into cocktail glasses and serve immediately.

rhubarb, strawberry, and white rum chiller

serves 2

6 strawberries
2 fluid ounces white rum
1 teaspoon natural vanilla extract
8 ice cubes

stewed rhubarb
7 stems rhubarb (about 10 1/2 ounces)
1/4 cup superfine sugar

To make the stewed rhubarb, trim the rhubarb stems and cut them into four pieces. Put the rhubarb, sugar, and 1/4 cup of water in a stainless steel saucepan over medium heat. Cover and simmer for 10 minutes. Remove from the heat and allow to cool.

Put the stewed rhubarb, strawberries, white rum, vanilla extract, and ice cubes in a blender and blend until smooth. Pour into chilled glasses.

bellini

1/2 **ripe white peach**
1 teaspoon superfine sugar
champagne

Puree the peach and sugar and set aside. Pour a little champagne into two champagne flutes and divide the peach puree between the glasses. Lightly stir. Top off with champagne.

cosmopolitan

ice cubes
2 fluid ounces vodka
1 fluid ounce Cointreau
1 teaspoon lime juice
2 tablespoons cranberry juice

Fill a cocktail shaker with ice cubes and add the vodka, Cointreau, lime juice, and cranberry juice. Shake vigorously, then strain into a chilled cocktail glass.

champagne cocktail   serves 1

1 sugar cube
3 dashes Angostura bitters
1/2 fluid ounce brandy
champagne

Moisten the sugar cube with the bitters and put in a champagne flute. Pour in the brandy and top with champagne.

watermelon, mint, and vodka

2 sprigs mint
5 watermelon juice ice cubes
1/2 cup watermelon juice
1/2 teaspoon lime juice
1 fluid ounce vodka

Put the mint sprigs and the watermelon ice cubes in a tall glass and pour over the watermelon juice, lime juice, and vodka. Stir well.

campari classic

¹/₂ cup orange juice
2 fluid ounces Campari
6 ice cubes
sliced orange, to garnish

Pour the orange juice and Campari into a tall glass and top with the ice cubes. Garnish with sliced orange.

sour cherry blossom   serves 2

ice cubes
1 tablespoon light whipping cream
2 fluid ounces gin
1/4 cup sour cherry nectar
1 egg white
1/4 fluid ounce framboise

Put the cream, gin, sour cherry nectar, egg white, and framboise into a shaker half-filled with ice cubes. Shake vigorously and pour into small, chilled cocktail glasses.

whiskey sour   serves 1

ice cubes
2 fluid ounces whiskey
2 tablespoons lemon juice
1 teaspoon superfine sugar
1 egg white
ice cubes, to serve
1 maraschino cherry, to serve

Fill a cocktail shaker three-quarters full with ice cubes. Add the whiskey, lemon juice, sugar, and a dash of egg white. Shake well. Strain into a small cocktail glass containing ice cubes and a maraschino cherry.

brandy alexander   serves 1

1¹/₂ fluid ounces brandy
1 fluid ounce crème de cacao
1 tablespoon light whipping cream
3–4 ice cubes
sprinkle of nutmeg, to garnish

Put the brandy, crème de cacao, cream, and ice cubes in a cocktail shaker and shake vigorously several times. Pour into a cocktail glass and garnish with a sprinkle of nutmeg.

roasted tomato pasta sauce mushroom pasta sauce
homemade pasta pesto polenta homemade pizza dough
homemade focaccia vegetable stock chicken stock
veal stock fish stock roasted chicken roasted lamb
roast beef olive and basil stuffing for lamb roasted
sweet potato horseradish gremolata beef marinade
lamb marinade caponata rouille chili-lime sauce red
wine sauce short-crust tart shell short-crust

06 basics

chocolate frosting cardamom and rosewater syrup
roasted tomato pasta sauce mushroom pasta sauce
homemade pasta pesto polenta homemade pizza dough
homemade focaccia vegetable stock chicken stock veal
stock fish stock roasted chicken roasted lamb roast

roasted tomato pasta sauce

serves 4

6 plum tomatoes
10 basil leaves
1 garlic clove
2 tablespoons extra-virgin olive oil
1 teaspoon balsamic vinegar
1 teaspoon sugar

Preheat the oven to 400°F. Put the tomatoes on a cookie sheet and roast until the skins begin to blacken all over. Put the whole tomatoes, including the charred skin and any juices, into a food processor or blender with the basil, garlic, oil, balsamic vinegar, and sugar. Blend to form a thick sauce, thinning the tomato mixture with a little warm water if necessary.

Toss the sauce through warm pasta and serve with grated Parmesan cheese and a few basil leaves.

mushroom pasta sauce serves 4

2 tablespoons butter
1 crushed garlic clove
4 1/2 cups halved button mushrooms
2 large meadow mushrooms,
  roughly chopped
1 teaspoon thyme leaves
4 tablespoons white wine

Heat the butter in a large frying pan over medium heat and add the garlic and mushrooms. Sauté for 5 minutes, then add the thyme leaves and wine. Simmer for an additional 1 minute.

Toss the sauce through warm pasta and drizzle with oil. Add Parmesan cheese and toss to combine.

homemade pasta

makes enough pasta for 4 main servings

3$^{1}/_{4}$ cups all-purpose flour
$^{1}/_{2}$ teaspoon salt
4 eggs
heaping $^{1}/_{3}$ cup semolina flour

Put the all-purpose flour into a food processor with the salt. Add the eggs and process until the mixture begins to come together in a rough dough.

Place the dough on a lightly floured board and dust with the semolina flour. Knead until the dough is smooth. Divide the dough into four equal portions and wrap in plastic wrap. Refrigerate for 30 minutes.

Put the pasta dough through a pasta machine according to the manufacturer's instructions. Cut the pasta when it has reached the desired thickness, then set it on a clean surface liberally sprinkled with more semolina or all-purpose flour. Toss the pasta through your fingers to separate it, then lay it on a floured tray while you cut the remaining dough.

pesto

4 cups basil leaves
2¹/₂ cups Italian parsley, roughly
   chopped
1 cup grated Parmesan cheese
1 garlic clove
¹/₂ cup pine nuts, toasted
²/₃ cup olive oil

Put the basil, parsley, Parmesan, garlic, and pine nuts into a food processor or a mortar and pestle and blend or pound the mixture to make a thick paste.

Add the oil in a steady stream until the paste has a spoonable consistency.

If you want to keep your pesto, put it in a sterilized jar and add a layer of olive oil on top. This will prevent the surface of the pesto from oxidizing and turning brown. Keep the pesto in the refrigerator for up to 2 weeks.

polenta

1 teaspoon sea salt
2¹/₃ cups polenta
1 tablespoon butter, cut into cubes
1 cup grated Parmesan cheese
sea salt and freshly ground black
   pepper, to season

Bring 8 cups of water and the sea salt to a boil in a saucepan. Lower the heat to a simmer and slowly add the polenta in a steady stream, stirring with a whisk to blend it smoothly. Reduce the heat to low and, stirring occasionally, allow the polenta to cook for 30 minutes. The polenta is cooked when it begins to pull away from the sides of the saucepan. Stir the butter and Parmesan through. Season with sea salt and freshly ground black pepper and serve immediately.

homemade pizza dough

makes 1 quantity pizza dough or 2 medium pizza
bases, approximately 9 inches in diameter depending
on the preferred thickness

2 teaspoons dried yeast or 1/2 ounce
  fresh yeast
1 teaspoon sugar
2 cups all-purpose flour
1 egg
2 1/2 tablespoons milk
1 teaspoon sea salt
olive oil

Put the yeast into a small bowl with the sugar and 4 tablespoons warm water. Lightly stir to combine. Set aside for 10–15 minutes or until the mixture starts to froth. Sift the flour into a bowl and make a well in the center. Add the egg, milk, sea salt, and the yeast mixture. Gradually work the ingredients together to form a stiff dough.

Turn the dough out onto a floured surface and knead until smooth and elastic. Oil a large bowl with a little olive oil and put the dough in it. Rub a little more oil over the dough before covering it with a damp cloth. Put the bowl in a warm place for 2 hours until the dough doubles in size.

Preheat the oven to 400°F. Divide the dough in half and roll it out on a floured surface. Place the dough on two oiled cookie sheets and add your toppings. Bake for 15 minutes.

homemade focaccia   makes 1 loaf

3 2/3 cups all-purpose flour
pinch of sea salt
2 teaspoons dried yeast or 1/2 ounce
   fresh yeast
1 teaspoon sugar
3 tablespoons olive oil
2 tablespoons extra-virgin olive oil
1 tablespoon sea salt, for sprinkling

Put the flour into a large bowl with a good pinch of sea salt. Put the yeast in a small bowl with 1 cup warm water and the sugar. Set aside for 10 minutes. When the mixture has started to froth, add it to the flour along with the olive oil. Work the ingredients together to form a rough dough before turning out onto a floured board.

Knead the dough until it is smooth and elastic. Place in an oiled bowl and cover with a dishtowel. Leave the bowl in a warm place for 1 hour, until the dough doubles in size.

Preheat the oven to 400°F. Put the dough onto an oiled 13 1/2 x 9 1/2-inch cookie sheet and press it out until it covers the sheet. Use your fingers to make dimples in the dough and then drizzle with the extra-virgin olive oil and sprinkle with the sea salt. Allow to rise for an additional 20 minutes. Bake for 20 minutes or until the focaccia is cooked through and golden brown on top.

vegetable stock

2 tablespoons unsalted butter
2 garlic cloves, crushed
2 onions, roughly chopped
4 leeks, coarsely chopped
3 carrots, coarsely chopped
3 celery stalks, thickly sliced
1 fennel bulb, coarsely chopped
1 handful Italian parsley
2 sprigs thyme
2 black peppercorns

Put the butter, garlic, and onions into a large, heavy-based saucepan. Over medium heat, stir until the onion is soft and transparent. Add the leeks, carrots, celery stalks, fennel bulb, parsley, thyme, and peppercorns. Add 16 cups water and bring to a boil. Reduce the heat and simmer for 2 hours. Allow to cool. Strain into another saucepan, using the back of a large spoon to press the liquid from the vegetables. Bring the stock to a boil, then reduce the heat to a rolling boil until the stock is reduced by half.

chicken stock makes approximately 8 cups

1 whole fresh chicken
1 onion, sliced
2 celery stalks, sliced
1 leek, roughly chopped
1 bay leaf
a few sprigs Italian parsley
6 peppercorns

Fill a large heavy-based saucepan with 12 cups cold water. Cut a fresh chicken into several large pieces and put them into the saucepan.

Bring just to a boil, then reduce the heat to a simmer. Skim any fat from the surface, then add the onion, celery stalks, leek, bay leaf, parsley stalks, and peppercorns. Maintain the heat at a low simmer for 2 hours.

Strain the stock into a bowl and allow to cool. Using a large spoon, remove any fat that has risen to the surface. If a more concentrated flavor is required, return the chicken stock to a saucepan and simmer over low heat. If you are not using the stock immediately, cover and refrigerate or freeze it.

veal stock
makes approximately 8 cups

2¹/₄ pounds veal bones
2 tablespoons olive oil
2 chopped onions
3 garlic cloves
2 leeks, roughly chopped
2 celery stalks, sliced
2 large tomatoes, roughly chopped
1 bay leaf
6 black peppercorns

Preheat the oven to 400°F. Put the veal bones and olive oil into a large roasting pan, rub the oil over the bones, and bake for 30 minutes. Add the onions, garlic, leeks, celery stalks, and tomatoes to the pan. Continue baking for about 1 hour or until the bones are well browned.

Transfer the roasted bones and vegetables to a large heavy-based saucepan and cover with plenty of cold water. Bring to a boil over medium heat, then reduce the heat to a simmer. Skim any fat from the surface, then add the bay leaf and black peppercorns. Cook at a low simmer for 4 hours. Strain the stock into a bowl and allow to cool. Using a large spoon, remove any fat on the surface. Return the veal stock to a saucepan and simmer over low heat to reduce and concentrate the flavor.

fish stock

makes approximately 4 cups

2 1/4 pounds fish bones
1 onion, chopped
1 carrot, chopped
1 fennel bulb, sliced
2 celery stalks, sliced
a few sprigs thyme
a few sprigs parsley
4 black peppercorns

Put the fish bones into a large saucepan with 8 cups of water. Bring just to a boil, then reduce the heat and simmer for 20 minutes. Strain the liquid through a fine sieve into another saucepan to remove the bones and then add the onion, carrot, fennel, celery, thyme, parsley, and black peppercorns. Bring back to a boil, then reduce the heat and simmer for an additional 35 minutes. Strain into a bowl and allow to cool.

olive and basil stuffing
for lamb   makes enough for 1 leg of lamb

1/2 **cup pitted kalamata olives**
15 basil leaves
1 handful Italian parsley
2 garlic cloves
1 cup ground almonds

Put the olives, basil, parsley, garlic, and ground almonds into a food processor. Pulse once or twice to form a rough paste. Press the paste into a boned leg of lamb and use a skewer to keep the opening closed. Roast the lamb immediately.

roasted sweet potato serves 4

2 large orange sweet potatoes
1 tablespoon oil
sea salt and freshly ground black
  pepper

Preheat the oven to 350°F. Peel the sweet potatoes and cut them into chunks. Toss the potatoes in the oil. Season with a good sprinkling of sea salt and freshly ground black pepper. Spread the potato chunks out in a roasting pan in a single layer. Roast for 30 minutes or until the potato is browned and cooked through.

horseradish gremolata serves 4

3 tablespoons finely chopped
   Italian parsley
1 tablespoon finely grated lemon zest
1 tablespoon finely grated fresh
   horseradish root

Mix all the ingredients together in a bowl. Serve sprinkled over osso bucco or seared lamb chops just before serving.

beef marinade

serves 4

1 cup red wine
2 finely chopped garlic cloves
1/2 teaspoon finely chopped rosemary
1/2 cup olive oil

Put the wine into a bowl with the garlic, rosemary, and olive oil. Stir to mix. Add your chosen cuts of beef and gently toss so that the pieces are thoroughly coated in the mixture. Put in the refrigerator and marinate for 2–3 hours. Remove the beef from the marinade and season well with freshly ground black pepper. Cook on the barbecue or in a frying pan until the beef is cooked to taste. Remove from the heat and season with sea salt. Allow to rest for 5 minutes before serving.

lamb marinade

1/2 cup white wine
4 tablespoons olive oil
juice of 1 lemon
1 tablespoon fresh oregano
1 garlic clove, finely chopped

Put the white wine, olive oil, lemon juice, oregano, and garlic into a bowl. Add lamb chops, loin chops, or a boned leg of lamb to the marinade. Toss to thoroughly coat the pieces in the marinade. Marinate in the refrigerator for 2–3 hours. Cook the lamb until it is still a little pink in the center. Season with sea salt and freshly ground black pepper. Allow to rest for 5 minutes before serving.

rouille

1 thick slice sourdough bread
1 pinch saffron threads
1 red bell pepper, roasted and skinned
1/4 teaspoon paprika
2 garlic cloves
1/2 cup light olive oil
salt, to season

Tear the bread into pieces and place it in a bowl. Bring the saffron threads and 1/4 cup of water to a boil in a small saucepan and gently simmer for 1 minute. Pour the hot saffron water over the bread.

Allow the bread to soak in the water and then add it to a food processor or blender with the bell pepper, paprika, and garlic. Blend to form a smooth paste, then add the olive oil in a stream to give a thick consistency. Season with salt to taste.

caponata

serves 4

1 large eggplant, cut into 1/2-inch cubes
1/4 cup olive oil
1 garlic clove, crushed
1 red bell pepper, finely diced
1 teaspoon thyme
2 tablespoons tomato paste
1 tablespoon salted capers, rinsed and drained
2 tablespoons finely sliced green olives
1 tablespoon finely chopped anchovies
1 cup finely chopped parsley

Lightly salt the eggplant and leave it to drain in a colander for 20 minutes. Rinse and pat dry with paper towels. Heat the oil in a heavy-based saucepan over medium heat and add the garlic. Stir for 1 minute, then add the cubed eggplant. Cook, stirring occasionally, until the eggplant is just turning golden, then add the bell pepper, thyme leaves, tomato paste, and 1/2 cup of water. Reduce the heat and leave to simmer covered for 15 minutes. Then add the capers, olives, and anchovies. Allow to cool. Just before serving, fold in the parsley.

chili-lime sauce

makes approximately 3/4 cup

2/3 cup grated jaggery (or brown sugar)
1 tablespoon dried red chili flakes
2 tablespoons lime juice

Combine the jaggery with 2/3 cup of water in a heavy-based saucepan. Bring to a boil and boil for 3 minutes. Add the dried red chili flakes, stir through, then remove the sauce from the heat. Allow to cool before stirring in the lime juice. Serve with baked or barbecued fish, fresh spring rolls, or drizzled over broiled chicken.

red wine sauce   serves 4

1 tablespoon finely diced red onion
1 garlic clove, chopped
2 tablespoons finely chopped celery
2 tablespoons grated carrot
1 cup red wine
1 cup veal stock (also in basics)
2 tablespoons chilled diced butter

Put the onion, garlic, celery, carrot, and wine in a small saucepan over low heat. Simmer for 10 minutes, then strain into another saucepan and add the veal stock. Bring to a boil, then reduce the heat and simmer for 15 minutes or until the liquid has been reduced by half. Just before serving, stir or whisk in the butter. Serve with lamb or beef.

short-crust tart shell

makes 1 tart shell

1²/3 cups all-purpose flour
heaping 1/3 cup unsalted butter
1 tablespoon superfine sugar

Put the flour, butter, sugar, and a pinch of salt into a food processor and process for 1 minute. Add 2 tablespoons of chilled water and pulse until the mixture comes together. Wrap the dough in plastic wrap and chill for 30 minutes.

Roll the pastry out as thinly as possible—the easiest way to do this is to roll it out between two layers of plastic wrap. Line a greased 10-inch tart pan. Chill for 30 minutes.

Prick the base, line it with crumpled waxed paper, and fill with baking weights or uncooked rice. Place the pan in a preheated 350°F oven for 10 to 15 minutes or until the pastry looks cooked and dry. Remove and allow to cool.

Note—Unbaked tart shells that are not used immediately can be stored in the freezer for several weeks. Put the tart shell in a preheated oven directly from the freezer (there's no need to thaw the shell first).

short-crust tartlet shells

makes 36 tartlet shells

1²/₃ cup all-purpose flour
heaping ¹/₃ cup unsalted butter
pinch salt

Put the flour, butter, and salt into a food processor and process for 1 minute. Add 2 tablespoons of iced water and pulse until the mixture comes together. Wrap in plastic wrap and chill for 30 minutes. Roll the pastry out and cut into rounds. Put into greased muffin or tartlet pans and chill for an additional 30 minutes.

Prick the bases and fill with baking weights or uncooked rice before placing in a preheated 350°F oven for 7–10 minutes. Remove and allow to cool. To make a sweet pastry, add 1 tablespoon of superfine sugar or 1 teaspoon natural vanilla extract.

Note—Unbaked tart shells that are not used immediately can be stored in the freezer for several weeks. Place in a preheated oven directly from the freezer (it is not necessary to thaw the tart shells first).

chocolate frosting

2/3 cup chopped dark chocolate
1/2 cup heavy cream
1 tablespoon Frangelico
1 teaspoon ground cinnamon

To make the frosting, put the chocolate and cream into a small saucepan over very low heat. As the cream begins to get hot, remove the pan from the heat and stir the chocolate until it has melted into the cream to form a thick sauce. Stir in the liqueur and cinnamon and then set the mixture aside to cool a little before frosting your cake.

cardamom and rosewater
syrup

makes 1 cup

1/2 cup sugar
1 teaspoon lemon juice
5 cardamom pods, lightly crushed
1/2 teaspoon rosewater

Put the sugar, lemon juice, and cardamom pods in a small saucepan and add 1 cup of water. Bring slowly to a boil, making sure that the sugar dissolves completely, before reducing the heat and simmering for 5 minutes. Remove the syrup from the heat and stir in the rosewater. The syrup will keep for two weeks in the refrigerator.

glossary

baby mozzarella

These are small balls of mozzarella, often sold in their own whey. When fresh, they are soft and springy to the touch and taste distinctly milky. They are available from most delicatessens.

balsamic vinegar

Balsamic vinegar is a dark, fragrant, and sweetish aged vinegar made from grape juice.

basil

The most commonly used basil is the sweet or Genoa variety which is much favored in Italian cooking. Thai or holy basil is used in Thai and Southeast Asian dishes. To get the most out of basil leaves, they should always be torn, not chopped.

butter puff pastry

This is puff pastry made with butter rather than vegetable fat, giving it a much more buttery flavor than standard puff pastry.

capers

Capers are the green buds from a Mediterranean shrub, preserved in brine or salt. Salted capers have a firmer texture and are often smaller than those preserved in brine. Rinse away the brine or salt before using them. Capers are available from good delicatessens.

cardamom

A dried seed pod native to India. The inner seeds when crushed give off a sweet aroma. It is used whole or ground and can be found in the spice section of most supermarkets. Cardamom should be used sparingly, as it is quite strong.

chocolate

Couverture is the best quality chocolate to use. This bittersweet chocolate contains the highest percentage of cocoa butter. It is available from delicatessens and food stores. If you can't find chocolate of this standard, then use a good-quality eating chocolate.

Chinese black beans

These salted black beans can be found either vacuum-packed or in cans in Asian food stores.

chipotle chilies

These are available from delicatessens in cans where they are preserved in a smoky rich sauce, or they can be bought as smoked and dried chilies that need to be reconstituted in warm water prior to use.

ciabatta

Italian for "slipper," this loaf of bread is supposed to be in the shape of a shoe. Very light and with a porous texture, the Italians favor this loaf for sandwiches.

cream

Cream comes with differing fat contents. If it needs to be whipped, it must have a fat content higher than 35 percent. Light cream cannot be whipped.

crème fraîche

A naturally soured cream that is lighter than sour cream. It is available at gourmet food stores and some supermarkets.

dried porcini mushrooms

Dried porcini (cèpes) mushrooms can be found either in small packets or sold loose from a jar in delicatessens.

feta cheese

Feta is a white cheese made from sheep or goat milk. The cheese is salted and cut into blocks before being aged in its own whey. It must be kept in the whey or in oil during storage. Persian feta is creamy in style. Feta is commonly available.

Frangelico

A hazelnut-flavored Italian liqueur sold in a brown bottle shaped like a monk's robe.

Gruyère cheese

A firm cow's milk cheese with a smooth texture and natural rind. It has a nutty flavor and melts easily, making it perfect for tarts and gratins.

haloumi cheese

Haloumi is a semifirm sheep's milk cheese. It has a rubbery texture that becomes pleasantly soft and chewy when the cheese is broiled or fried. It is available from delicatessens and most large supermarkets.

haricot beans

Many types of beans belong to the haricot family, including cannellini (kidney-shaped beans) and flageolet (white or pale green beans), and also navy beans, which are famous for their use in baked beans. In Europe and the United States, kidney beans are also called white beans.

horseradish

Horseradish is a root of the mustard family—large and white, it has a knobbly brown skin. It is very pungent and has a spicy, hot flavor. Horseradish is usually freshly grated as a condiment for roast beef and smoked fish. When commercially produced, horseradish is often blended with cream to give it a smoother texture. Dollop on roast beef or smoked salmon.

Indian lime pickle

Lime pickle is available from Indian grocery stores or large supermarkets. It is usually served as a side dish.

jaggery

Jaggery is an unrefined sugar obtained from the sap of various palm trees and is sold in hard cakes and in plastic jars. If it is very hard it will need to be grated. It can be found in Asian grocery stores or supermarkets.

jalapeño chilies

Small pickled jalapeño chilies are available in jars in specialty stores and large supermarkets. They add a sweet but fiery bite to salsas and should be used to personal taste.

Marsala

Perhaps Italy's most famous fortified wine, Marsala is available in sweet and dry varieties. Often used in desserts such as zabaglione, it is a superb match with eggs, cream, and almonds.

mascarpone cheese

This heavy, Italian-style set cream is used as a base in many sweet and savory dishes. It is made from cream rather than milk, so it is high in fat. It can be eaten on its own, served simply with fruit. It is sold at delicatessens and supermarkets.

matsutake mushrooms

Also known as pine mushrooms, these Japanese mushrooms are brown in color and thick and meaty in texture. They are best if cooked simply by sautéing in butter with a little garlic.

mozzarella cheese

Fresh mozzarella can be found in most delicatessens and is easily identified by its smooth, white appearance and ball-like shape. It is not to be confused with mass-produced mozzarella, which is mostly used as a pizza topping. Mozzarella is usually sold packed in whey.

mustard seeds

Mustard seeds have a sharp, hot flavor that is tempered by cooking. Both brown and yellow are available, although brown mustard seeds are more common.

niçoise olives

Niçoise or Ligurian olives are small black olives that are used in salads or sprinkled over dishes. They are not suitable for pitting and making into pastes.

orzo

Orzo is small rice-shaped pasta. It is ideal for use in soups or salads where its small shape is able to absorb the other flavors of the dish.

pancetta

Pancetta is salted belly of pork. It is sold in delicatessens, especially Italian ones, and some supermarkets. Pancetta is available either rolled and thinly sliced or in large pieces ready to be diced or cut. It adds a rich bacon flavor to dishes.

panettone
An aromatic Italian yeast bread made with raisins and candied peel, panettone is traditionally eaten at Christmas. They are available in large and small sizes.

pesto
Available in most supermarkets, pesto is a pureed sauce traditionally made from basil, garlic, Parmesan cheese, pine nuts, and olive oil.

pomegranate molasses
This is a thick syrup made from the reduction of pomegranate juice. It has a bittersweet flavor, which adds a sour bite to many Middle Eastern dishes. It is available from Middle Eastern specialty stores.

preserved lemon
These are whole lemons preserved in salt or brine for about 30 days, which turns their rind soft and pliable. Just the rind is used—the pulp should be scraped out and thrown away. Preserved lemon is an ingredient commonly found in Moroccan cooking. It is available from delicatessens.

prosciutto
Prosciutto is lightly salted, air-dried ham. It is most commonly bought in paper-thin slices and is available from delicatessens and large supermarkets. Parma ham and San Daniele are both types of prosciutto.

ricotta cheese
Ricotta cheese can be bought cut from a wheel or in tubs. The wheel tends to be firmer in consistency and is better for baking. If you can only get ricotta in tubs, drain off any excess moisture by letting it sit for a couple of hours in a sieve lined with cheesecloth.

risotto rice
Three well-known varieties of risotto rice are widely available today: *arborio,* a large plump grain that makes a sticky risotto; *vialone nano,* a shorter grain that gives a loose consistency but keeps more of a bite in the middle; and *carnaroli,* similar in size to vialone nano, but which makes a risotto with a firm consistency. All three types are interchangeable, although cooking times may vary by 5 minutes or so.

rosewater
The distilled essence of rose petals, rosewater is used in small quantities to impart a perfumed flavor to pastries, fruit salads, and sweet puddings. It is available from delicatessens and large supermarkets.

saffron threads

These are the orange-red stigmas from one species of the crocus plant, and the most expensive spice in the world. Saffron should be bought in small quantities and used sparingly—not only due to the cost but as it has a very strong flavor.

smoked paprika

Paprika is commonly sold as a dried, rich red powder made from a member of the chili family. It comes in many grades from delicate to sweet and finally hot. Smoked paprika from Spain adds a distinct rich and smoky flavor to dishes.

sour cherries and cherry nectar

These bottled, European-style morello cherries are commonly sold in jars. Both the juice and the fruit are used in cooking. Sour cherry nectar is available in cartons from most large supermarkets.

sterilizing jars

It's always a good idea to sterilize jars or bottles before filling with food that you may intend to keep for a while. To do so, wash the jar in hot soapy water, boil for 10 minutes in a large saucepan, then drain on a clean dishtowel. Dry in a 250°F oven and then remove and fill while the jars are still hot.

tortillas

This thin, round, unleavened bread is used in Mexican cooking as a wrap. Tortillas are available prepackaged in the refrigerator section of most supermarkets.

vanilla

The long, slim, black vanilla bean has a wonderful caramel aroma that synthetic vanillas can never capture. Store unused vanilla pods in a full jar of superfine sugar, which will not only help to keep the vanilla fresh but the aroma of the bean will infuse the sugar, making it ideal for use in baking.

vine leaves

The large, green leaves of the grapevine are available packed in cans, jars, or in brine. The leaves are used in Greek and Middle Eastern cuisine to wrap foods for cooking. Vine leaves in brine should be rinsed before use.

wonton wrappers

These paper-thin sheets of dough are available fresh or frozen from Asian grocery stores. They can be wrapped around fillings and steamed, deep-fried, or used in broths, and come shaped as squares and circles.

index